FOR THIS HE CAME

*Jesus' Journey
to the Cross*

Also by Bill Crowder

Let's Talk

Seeing the Heart of Christ (forthcoming)

Singing the Songs of the Brokenhearted

The Spotlight of Faith

Windows on Christmas

Windows on Easter

FOR THIS HE CAME

Jesus' Journey to the Cross

Bill Crowder

Discovery House®
from Our Daily Bread Ministries

Formerly published as *The Path of His Passion*

Discovery House is affiliated with Our Daily Bread Ministries,
Grand Rapids, Michigan.

Requests for permission to quote from this book should be directed to:
Permissions Department, Discovery House, P.O. Box 3566, Grand
Rapids, MI 49501, or contact us by email at permissionsdept@dhp.org.

Unless otherwise indicated, Scripture quotations are from the
New American Standard Bible®, © 1960, 1962, 1963, 1968, 1971,
1972, 1973, 1975, 1977, 1995 by The Lockman Foundation.
Used by permission. (Lockman.org)

ISBN: 978-1-62707-907-5

Printed in the United States of America

First printing of this edition in 2018

To my parents, Earl and Bee Crowder:
For your encouragement and love, for your example
and character, for your wisdom and care. Thanks.

CONTENTS

Acknowledgments 9

Foreword 11

PART ONE: PREPARATION

One: Impressions from an Upper Room 15

Two: On the Road to Gethsemane 35

Three: Alone in the Garden 55

PART TWO: CONDEMNATION

Four: Betrayed by a Friend 73

Five: Denied by a Friend 91

Six: Tried by His Enemies 107

Seven: Surrounded by the Crowd 123

PART THREE: SALVATION

Eight: The Mockery of Calvary 143

Nine: The Majesty of Calvary 159

Ten: The Victory of Calvary 175

PART FOUR: EXALTATION

Eleven: The Return to the Father 197

Conclusion 217

ACKNOWLEDGMENTS

Once again I find myself completely overwhelmed with the level of teamwork, support, skill, and encouragement necessary to complete a project like this. It is nothing short of hard work—but it is also a labor of love. In part, it is a labor of love because of the subject. The work of Christ in going to Calvary to die for me is an amazing thing. To study it is to attempt to plumb the depths of the love of God Himself. It is an awesome exercise, and I am humbled to have been entrusted with this privilege. I cannot believe that I would be permitted to write a book like this, and I am grateful.

Second, it is a labor of love because of the team I am privileged to work with at Discovery House. My deepest thanks to Carol Holquist and the publishing committee for saying yes to this project. I stand in awe of Judy Markham and Annette Selden and their editorial skills—and want to express my thanks to and my dependence on them in making my heart readable in a book like this. For the whole DH crew—Bob DeVries, Kathy Comer, Melissa Wade, Kim Fowler, and Judy Grothause—you guys are the best! Thanks for making this possible and for believing in it. A special thanks as well to Peggy Willison, whose skill in proofreading helps us do good stuff with excellence.

Also, it is a labor of love because of the support structure the Lord has given me at home. From my mom, who still is pretty tickled I stepped into a pulpit, to my kids (Matt, Steve and Kim, Beth and Brian, Andy and Katie, Mark and Amy), who understand when I sit with my computer in my lap and the world fades into the background—and are even nice about it. Especially to my bride of more than forty years, Marlene. For all these years she has acted like she really believes I can do anything—even when I have no idea what the next step is. Marlene has been the greatest partner God could have ever given me for the journey.

Mostly, it has been a labor of love because of the joy and wonder I have felt in my own heart once again as I have tried to understand what it meant for the King of heaven to do what He did for me—"Jesus, the author and perfecter of faith, who for the joy set before Him endured the cross, despising the shame, and has sat down at the right hand of the throne of God" (Hebrews 12:2). "Amazing love, how can it be, that Thou my God shouldst die for me?"

FOREWORD

When I was a boy, my father took me to the Alban Theater in St. Albans, West Virginia, to see the movie *King of Kings* about the life of Jesus Christ. As a kid, it was pretty difficult for me to comprehend what it all meant. Years later, as a student in Bible college, I heard an evangelist preach what remains to this day the most powerful message I have ever heard on the suffering of Christ on the cross—and was moved in ways I had never imagined possible. Once I entered pastoral ministry, I felt the deep personal need to try to understand the sufferings of Christ for the sins of the world, so I preached a series of messages that lasted for twelve weeks of Sunday mornings on that powerful theme. During the study and preparation for those messages, my comprehension of the agonies of the Savior grew a little bit more. In 2004, with the release of Mel Gibson's film *The Passion of the Christ*, I felt that what I had "seen" in years of study was being presented before my eyes, and I understood a little more.

After thirty years of walking with Christ, I don't believe I fully understand all that Christ suffered for me or what it meant for Him to do that, but I find myself more determined than ever to try to embrace the cross that Christ embraced for me. Join me in the journey of seeking Him, considering Him, worshiping Him—of walking with Him along the path of His passion. I believe it will be worth it, for we will see Him—and that is all that matters.

PART ONE:

PREPARATION

ONE

IMPRESSIONS FROM AN UPPER ROOM

I t is a little foggy in my mind, but it seems I was about eight or nine years old. It was a Sunday morning, and I was sitting in the balcony of the church with my brother. My parents were both seated in the choir, so they were keeping an eye on me from that remarkably clear vantage point. None of this was terribly unusual. What turned the page on that morning was when the Communion portion of the worship service began. The ushers came with the plates of little cubes cut from a loaf of Wonder bread, and, like everyone else, we each took a piece and waited for the instructions to eat. It was quiet and somber. So far so good.

It was at this point that something happened. Maybe I have simply blocked it from my memory, but, for the life of me, I can't remember what actually caused us to start laughing. Nonetheless, we got tickled and started laughing and just couldn't stop! By the time the juice tray came, we were such a mess that we actually spilled it as it passed by—and that was enough to jar us back to reality. Everyone in the balcony turned to show their displeasure with these two delinquents. The usher burned a pretty good hole in my head with his laser-beam eyes. And my brother and I looked sheepish. We were thoroughly embarrassed, and deserved to be. Then I looked down to the choir loft and saw the expression on my dad's face. In that instant, my emotional framework changed from embarrassment to terror. I honestly believed, as only a little kid caught in a bad situation can, that my life would soon be coming to an end—if not in the church parking lot, certainly when we got home.

It may have been the only time as a kid that I didn't want church to end. When it did, I ran to the car and got in the far back seat of our Plymouth station wagon and hoped that somehow Dad would be distracted and forget what had happened. He didn't. The good news (as attested by the fact that I am here to tell this story) is that I didn't die that day. What did happen, in addition to some punishment that will remain undescribed, was that my dad gave me a very long, very stern, and very appropriate talking-to about the seriousness of the Communion table. Frankly, I didn't understand a lot of the things my dad was saying any more than I had understood it an hour or so earlier when the pastor said it. I didn't understand the symbolism or the meaning or the purpose. None of it. What I did get very clearly, however, is that the Lord's Supper is not something that you play around with—it is very serious. It deals with serious issues in very serious ways. That part I understood. My dad made sure of it.

I wonder if that is somehow similar to the thinking and feeling of the disciples of Jesus as they gathered in the upper room, expecting a feast of celebration and finding that the Master turned the evening into a very somber event. The events transformed from lighthearted festivity to murky symbols and serious words—symbols and words that they did not begin to fully comprehend. Symbols and words that we continue to struggle with in both their meaning and their implications. I think it is extremely valuable to consider those symbols and words and the events that surrounded them as we consider that night—the night before the Cross. Those symbols and words carry great weight, and we must be very careful about how we approach them. Our journey through the passion does not begin at the foot of the cross, at the courts of trial, or even in a dark garden where Christ would agonize in prayer. No, the path of the suffering of Christ begins at a party—a memorial feast that would become Christ's own.

THE ROAD TO THE PASSOVER

As we join the story, Jesus has been involved in public ministry for about three years. His public ministry began when He presented Himself to John the Baptist for baptism and then endured the testing of the wilderness at the hand of the Enemy. The following period of public ministry included the selection and training of disciples, public preaching and teaching, and the powerful display of miracles that impacted the physical, natural, and spiritual worlds. (The Bible is not specific about the time frame of these events, but we can get a rough chronology by the recorded Passovers in Jesus' ministry—Passover feasts that also pointed to the events of Christ's suffering.)

Now the time has come to celebrate the Passover, and it marks the third recorded Passover of Christ's ministry. The days of His public efforts are over. The triumphal entry and the cleansing of the temple have been accomplished. The final moments of Jesus' earthly ministry are rushing to their climax at breakneck speed. During the Passion Week, Christ has spent His days teaching in the temple in Jerusalem and apparently has spent His evenings resting in the home of His friend Lazarus at nearby Bethany. It has been a rigorous and challenging week as Christ has enthralled the crowds and enraged the religious establishment with His teaching.

This Passover, however, will be distinctly different from the other two. This will be the only time that Jesus Himself offers the sacrifice and leads the worship as the head of a group.

- In the first Passover of the public ministry of Christ, He had not yet assembled all of His disciples. Because a group of at least ten men was required to celebrate, Christ could not lead such a feast (John 2:13, 23).

- Jesus sent His disciples ahead to Jerusalem for their second Passover pilgrimage but did not join them there (John 6:1, 7:1). (Some scholars see another Passover feast in John 5:1, but it is not conclusive.)

This Passover will be different—not only from the other two during Christ's season of public ministry, but different from any Passover that has ever been shared. It will not only be different because Jesus will lead it but also because of the events it will foreshadow in both symbols and words. Jesus will take the ancient feast and transform it from an historic remembrance to a prophetic event. He will build on the Israelite portrait of the events that produced liberation from slavery in Egypt and will create from it a portrait of the next few hours—hours that will result in rescue from the bondage of sin. The disciples are looking back to the Exodus and are ready to party, but Jesus is looking ahead to Golgotha and is ready to give them one of the most significant lessons of their time together.

SETTING THE STAGE FOR A CELEBRATION

In West Michigan, which we have now called home for twenty-seven years, there is a tradition attached to high school graduation: the graduation open house. Frankly, it is a lot of work, but it's what you do. Weeks ahead of the graduation ceremony, a date is selected and invitations are prepared. A menu is planned and food is purchased. Decorations are bought and a photomontage of the honored graduate is assembled. In the twenty-seven years that my wife and I have been attending numerous open houses, we have observed that the menu varies (though it usually includes at least one cake, a veggie tray, meatballs in a crock pot, and maybe some of those really good little cocktail weenies in barbecue sauce) and the location can vary (sometimes in the home, sometimes in the church fellowship hall). What doesn't vary is the amount of work parents do to put one of these shindigs on. I know—we have hosted five. The moral of the story? Putting on a party is no party!

This was especially true with the celebration feast of Passover. In addition to issues of location and food preparation, there was an extremely stringent element—the religious guidelines of Judaism rooted in the Old Testament Scriptures, which contained strict rules for the preparation and celebration of the rescue meal. It was a pile of work, especially when, as was the case in the Passover celebrated by Jesus and His men, it was being observed in a city far from home. The logistics were challenging, to say the least, because of the significance of the celebration.

Understanding the Feast

The Passover began in the book of Exodus when God Himself powerfully delivered the children of Israel after about four hundred years of slavery in Egypt. The Hebrews had come to Egypt as welcome guests of Pharaoh during a time of famine. Joseph, a Hebrew slave who had become "prime minister" of Egypt, had brought his family to a place of provision so that he could care for them, and they stayed. After a period of time, there arose a pharaoh who "knew not Joseph," and, seeing the burgeoning numbers of Israelites as an internal security threat, he placed them in bondage, forcing them to build the cities of Egypt out of bricks and mortar. After centuries of suffering, God rescued them by the hand of Moses through a series of supernatural events that convinced the pharoah to let God's people go.

The final event of these divine acts of deliverance was the threatened death of the firstborn of all the land. Hebrew and Egyptian alike were vulnerable to the threat, and Hebrew and Egyptian alike had the opportunity to make use of the prescribed prevention of that death. A lamb was to be slaughtered and its blood placed on the doorposts (side supports) and lintel (door header) of the house. When God's emissary of death saw the blood, he would "pass over" (Exodus 12:1–14). From that night of death and deliverance on, the children of Israel would celebrate Passover with the same elements of the feast that had been used in Egypt.

Passover was one of the high feasts of Israel and contained a number of elements, highlighted by the actual Seder (Passover) dinner itself. The entire event was the Feast of Unleavened Bread, an eight-day period beginning on the fourteenth of Nisan (which corresponds with our March/April). For these eight days, the Jewish people were to eat unleavened bread as a symbol of personal purging and cleansing of sin. This picture was significant, because throughout much of the Bible, leaven (yeast) is symbolic of sin. As the Jews ate this flat, often tasteless, bread, it was a reminder of the explosive and combustible potential of sin when it enters the human heart.

As this most significant Passover comes upon Jesus and His men, it is introduced in Matthew 26:17: "Now on the first day of Unleavened Bread the disciples came to Jesus and asked, 'Where do You want us to prepare for You to eat the Passover?'"

With the coming of the Feast of Unleavened Bread, it is time for the preparations of Passover to begin.

Securing a Location

And He said, "Go into the city to a certain man, and say to him, 'The Teacher says, "My time is near; I am to keep the Passover at your house with My disciples"'" (Matthew 26:18).

The first issue to be resolved was the site for their feast. As men of Galilee, they would not have had homes in Jerusalem. As men of modest means, they would not have had extraordinary resources at their disposal. When the disciples asked Jesus where they should prepare the feast, He offered a unique solution to the problem. He instructed them to go to "a certain man." Jerusalem was teeming with people, and all were there for the feast! What would set apart this "certain man" from all the rest? Matthew didn't answer the question, but Luke did. In his record of the events, the apostolic physician said:

And Jesus sent Peter and John, saying, "Go and prepare the Passover for us, so that we may eat it." They said to Him, "Where do You want us to prepare it?" And He said to them, "When you have entered the city, a man will meet you carrying a pitcher of water; follow him into the house that he enters. And you shall say to the owner of the house, 'The Teacher says to you, "Where is the guest room in which I may eat the Passover with My disciples?"' And he will show you a large, furnished upper room; prepare it there." And they left and found everything just as He had told them; and they prepared the Passover (Luke 22:8–13).

To the Western eye, this would not appear to narrow things down very much. For the Jew in the first century, however, it was all the information needed. The key element of Jesus' instructions came when He said, "A man will meet you carrying a pitcher of water," for this would have been quite unusual. Fetching water was considered to be a woman's task, so men would have very seldom been seen carrying a water pot. Giving Jesus' instructions in more detail than Matthew, Luke records that they were to follow this man to an "upper room" and to prepare the feast there. Needless to say, it all occurred just as the Master had told them. It is also of note that Peter and John, the disciples closest to Jesus, were the ones selected for the honor—and the work!—of preparing for the Passover meal. They followed this "certain man" to the upper room Jesus had spoken of and set about the business of preparing the meal.

The fact that it was an *upper* room is worth noting. Most houses in that day were single-story boxes with flat roofs and outside stairways leading to a rooftop deck. The deck was like an extra living space that could give some cooling relief from the heat of the house in the evenings. This house went beyond, having an actual room as the second story. Two things bear consideration:

- This may have been the home of a young John Mark, who would have heard the group leave later that evening and followed them to Gethsemane—witnessing the betrayal and arrest of the Lord and fleeing into the night, leaving his sleep clothes behind and then recounting the story in his gospel record (Mark 14:51–52).
- This was undoubtedly the same upper room (Acts 1:13) that would later serve as a haven for the fearful disciples following Christ's death and burial and the place where they later gathered and received the Holy Spirit in anticipation of the day of Pentecost.

So, having their instructions, Peter and John separate from the rest of the disciples and make their way to find the man with the water jug. It is also likely that, at least at first, Judas accompanies them. Judas carried "the bag" (John 12:6) that held the group's finances and that would have been needed to purchase the necessary supplies for the meal. Now the wheels are beginning to be set in motion.

Preparing the Elements

The disciples did as Jesus had directed them; and they prepared the Passover (Matthew 26:19).

It is interesting that Matthew, writing his gospel record to a primarily Jewish audience, felt no need to go into any details about the preparations. He just flatly stated that those preparations were made. For our purposes, it would be useful to understand all that was involved. There would have been several steps for Peter and John in setting the room for the anticipated "party," including:

1. Going to the temple to purchase a pure sacrificial lamb, no doubt at horribly inflated prices, also involving the need to convert their normal money into temple currency at a ridiculous exchange rate. (Just days before, Jesus had cleansed the temple of the marketplace mentality it had assumed, but now the Father's house was once again a money-making machine.)
2. Slaughtering the lamb in a mass ceremony under the direction of the priests at 3:00 p.m. (Bible scholars estimate that in that one day some 250,000 lambs would be sacrificed.)

3. Catching the blood of the slaughtered lamb in a bowl and pouring it on an altar while singing, "O LORD, do save, we beseech You; O LORD, we beseech You, do send prosperity! Blessed is the one who comes in the name of the LORD" (Psalm 118:25–26).
4. Roasting the lamb on the altar and bringing it to the upper room for the feast.
5. Preparing the other items of the feast—each very symbolic in its own right—after returning to the upper room. The unleavened bread pictured sinlessness. The bitter herbs were to remind the Jewish people of their bitter slavery in Egypt and God's rescue. The sauce (*charosheth*) was a paste made of figs, nuts, almonds, vinegar, and herbs, symbolizing the mortar used on the bricks in their Egyptian slavery.

Nothing is left to chance. Nothing is superfluous. Every element of the feast is intended to picture something else, with the centerpiece of the meal—the lamb—ultimately picturing the Lamb of God who would in just a few hours take away the sins of the world (John 1:29). All the elements are prepared, meaning that all the pictures are in place and ready for the Lamb to come and make the feast His own memorial supper.

ALTERING THE MOOD OF A CELEBRATION

The first time I led a teaching trip to Israel was a dream come true for me. We traveled up the coast of the Mediterranean Sea and visited Megiddo and the Galilee. We journeyed south down through the Jordan valley and saw the wonder of Beth-Shean, a huge archaeological dig, before stopping at the oasis of Jericho. We then made our way to the crown jewel of Israel, Jerusalem, the city of peace.

On our first day touring the Old City, one of our stops was at the traditional site of the upper room. The architecture was more Byzantine than first-century Jewish, but it's the thought that counts, so we went in.

There were several groups from around the country that had been combined by the tour agency with our little band to make a busload, so we were a bit of a mixed multitude as we worked our way up the narrow staircase to the "room." Once there, we found it was already full of other tour groups that had been drawn to the Bible lands from all over the world, most softly praying or discussing the events of the Last Supper. At that moment, some folks began to sing "Amazing Grace." It was tender, heartfelt, and sweet, and the other tour groups in the room hushed or joined in. When the verse was over, there were soft amens around the room, and all went back to their own meditations.

Unfortunately, the singers had only begun. They continued, growing louder and louder until none of the other groups could even hear each other speak. As several tour guides came and asked the singers to respect the other groups, they relentlessly went on with their concert until all the verses of the old hymn had been spent. Smugly satisfied that they had won the day, the singers marched out triumphantly, consigning to hell two Jewish guides who had questioned their right to so rudely disrupt the upper room. Talk about altering the mood of a moment! The atmosphere in the upper room went from quiet worship and simple prayerfulness to belligerent, combative, un-Christlike attitudes in a matter of nanoseconds. It was a sad time that hung like a dark cloud over our little group for the rest of the day.

In a similar way, the expectations and emotions of the disciples would be quickly unsettled in their upper room experience as well. They were all set for a party and a celebration, but the moment they would reach the prepared place, it would become apparent to them that this would not be the normal, run-of-the-mill Passover. The mood was different. Something was not quite right. Something felt—wrong. Out of place. Disturbing and disturbed.

The disciples made their way with the Christ from Bethany into the city, within the walls of Jerusalem and within reach of danger itself for the Master. They navigated through the darkened streets and arrived at the upper room. Everything was set, and the disciples must have been experiencing an emotional high. In their eyes, Jesus' popularity was at an all-time high. The triumphal entry, the acclaim of the people as Christ taught in the temple, and the victories He easily won in debate with the religious leaders would have combined to create a sense of invulnerability—but not for long. Everything was about to change.

A Change in Roles

Jesus, knowing that the Father had given all things into His hands, and that He had come forth from God and was going back to God, got up from supper, and laid aside His garments; and taking a towel, He girded Himself. Then He poured water into the basin, and began to wash the disciples' feet and to wipe them with the towel with which He was girded (John 13:3–5).

According to culture, Jesus, as the leader of the group, could have rightly expected someone to wash His feet in preparation for the feast. It was customary to provide this service to guests for several reasons. It was certainly refreshing in a hot and dusty climate. More importantly, though, meals were eaten in a reclining position—which meant that it was possible that your feet might be at someone else's head. Couple this dining style with the reality that first-century Israel did not have modern sewage facilities (refuse and raw sewage were often dumped into the streets), and it was likely that those feet had been walking through some pretty unappetizing stuff. Foot washing was not only a cultural expectation, it was a practical necessity.

Still, none of the disciples rose to wash the Savior's feet. This was a job usually forced upon the lowest servant in the household—and no one wanted to sign up for that. In fact, in only a matter of a couple of hours, these men would be once again arguing over who was the greatest. After a deliberate period of time, Jesus Himself took the towel and the basin and began to wash their feet. Instantly, the mood in the room changed. The Master had become the Servant. The Lord had taken the role of a slave. This was a party no more—something different was going on.

A Change of Heart

As Jesus approached, Peter, the ever-popular "apostle of the foot-shaped mouth," pulled his legs under him and refused to let Jesus wash his feet.

> So He came to Simon Peter. He said to Him, "Lord, do You wash my feet?" Jesus answered and said to him, "What I do you do not realize now, but you will understand hereafter." Peter said to Him, "Never shall You wash my feet!" Jesus answered him, "If I do not wash you, you have no part with Me." Simon Peter said to Him, "Lord, then wash not only my feet, but also my hands and my head." Jesus said to him, "He who has bathed needs only to wash his feet, but is completely clean; and you are clean, but not all of you" (John 13:6–10).

The imagery of servanthood had overwhelmed Peter, and he would not allow the Lord to serve him. It was not humility as much as pride that drove Peter's resistance. "You'll never wash my feet!" Christ immediately drove home the point of the exercise. It wasn't about having clean feet; it was about having a clean heart—a heart that was continually being cleansed by the ongoing work of the Savior. It was intended to serve as the symbolic equivalent of 1 John 1:9: "If we confess our sins, He is faithful and righteous to forgive us our sins and to cleanse us from all unrighteousness."

The point? As we confess our sins to Christ, He provides the cleansing that allows our relationship with the Father to be unhindered. But we must be willing to humble ourselves before Him and submit to His cleansing and His Word. Peter's salvation had been cared for, secured when he gave his life to Christ. Foot washing was to picture the ongoing, day-to-day relationship of walking with God through a filth-laden world.

Immediately, Peter's emotional pendulum swung to the other extreme—"Not just my feet then! Wash me all over!" Christ's response was direct and plain: "No. That has already been resolved. It is the ongoing cleansing of the dirt of the world that is needed." Peter submitted—as we must submit—to the cleansing of Christ, and the celebration, albeit a very different celebration from the one the disciples had anticipated when they entered the upper room, could now begin. That celebration, like the mood of the room and its occupants, would also need to be changed.

CHANGING THE MEANING OF A CELEBRATION

The Passover had stood for hundreds of years to point the hearts of the Israelites back to their jubilee of rescue from the other side of the Nile. It would now focus on a different point of rescue. As Christ led His men through the ritual, all the parts had meaning, and each message was profound. Now Christ would make this His own—not to point the eyes of Israel back to bricks and mortar and chains, but to point the eyes of the world back to the Cross. The King introduced this as the ritualistic steps of the feast unfolded under His direction.

1. Jesus gave thanks for symbols that represented His coming crucifixion and shared the first of four cups prepared for the feast. Each of those cups was linked to a promise in Exodus 6:6–7. The promise of the first cup? "I will bring you out from under the burden of the Egyptians." Then, Jesus offered the prayer of blessing: "Blessed are You, O Lord, King of the universe, who brings forth bread from the earth."

2. To remind those present of the hardness and bitterness of the years of slavery in Egypt, Jesus introduced the element of the bitter herbs.

3. Next, He presented the unleavened bread and the sacrificed lamb as the focal points of the feast.

4. Jesus and the disciples dipped the bitter herbs in vinegar and ate them.

5. The next step involved the preparation of the wine, which, in a Jewish household, would prompt the youngest son to ask the ritual question, "Why is this night different from other nights?"

6. The group then sang Psalms 113 and 114 before drinking the second cup, linked to the promise, "I will rescue you from their bondage."

7. As recorded in John 13, Jesus then washed His hands and prepared the "sop" as the disciples ate the herbs. As the Master washed His hands, He then hit them with a thunderbolt of information for which they were completely unprepared. "One of you will betray Me!" (vv. 20–21). The disciples' world turned on this moment as they began to struggle with the implications of Christ's words. "One of us? A traitor? How can it be? Who can it be?"

As the realization of betrayal sank in, the Eleven responded with an appropriate lack of self-trust: "Lord, is it I?" Each one somehow understood that he was actually capable of such a thing, and each feared that he might be the one to sell out the Savior. By contrast, Judas, perhaps to test Christ and see if He already knew of his arrangement with the Pharisees, also asked, "Teacher is it I?" (v. 25), but in a shameless hypocrisy that sought to hide behind the mask of concern. If He were testing Christ to see if He knew, the answer would become brutally clear—He did! Jesus reveals this knowledge of His betrayer when John (at Peter's request) asks, "Lord, who is it?" (vv. 24–25).

Jesus answers John that the betrayer is "the one to whom I give the sop." In the first of several pictures of grace that Christ would continue to extend to Judas throughout this long, dark night, the Master gives the sop—a portion of bread wrapped around a piece of lamb, bitter herbs, and one radish (all of which spoke of the coming suffering of the Savior)—to Iscariot. What makes this a picture of grace? Traditionally, the head of the group gave the sop to the guest of honor at the feast! Here is grace freely offered to the one who had agreed to sell the Son for the price of a slave.

Judas, in an act of treachery, accepts the sop—giving the appearance of acceptance without the reality of acceptance—then leaves the group, the upper room, and the presence of the Lord. He departs to complete the act of treachery Jesus had just exposed and "goes out into the night." One of the greatest pictures of human tragedy in the Scriptures, Judas Iscariot symbolizes wasted opportunity, rejected grace, and unaccepted love. Fatal choices all.

The sop is now passed for all to share in, but the atmosphere has changed! It is no longer a festive celebration, but the foreboding beginnings of a wake. These men are now saddened by the heartbreaking news of the presence of a traitor in their midst. In fact, they are so stunned by these events that, for this moment, their arguing is silenced and their grasping for position and power is stymied by the significance of the sudden turn their night has taken.

I find it extremely significant that the disciples had no clue that the traitor was Judas! We have caricatured Judas as the evil-looking, dark, sinister presence among the apostolic band, but that simply was not the case. He blended in with the rest, looking and acting like the others. He was so much an accepted part of the team that it is even possible that Judas was the last one they would have expected! This probably was because Jesus showed Judas no less grace, no less love, and no less mercy than He did anyone else in the group, though He knew all along that Judas would betray Him.

Calvary is now less than twenty-four hours away, and already the weight of the cross burdens the Lord's shoulders. Yet, in this moment and over the ashes of a dying feast, Jesus presents us His monument—not in stone or marble, but in bread and wine. The mood in the upper room is somber and reflective—as ours should be any time that we approach His table and reflect on that monument. Why?

- Because *all* Passovers were celebrated in the shadow of the Cross—a place we must learn to live as well.

- Because *all* of us have the capacity to betray the Savior—which should drive us to our knees in dependence upon Him.

- Because *all* of us have at one time or another denied Him in word or thought or deed and must deal with that in confession as we view the table of His cross.

This explains why Paul, in 1 Corinthians 11:23–31, issues warnings to the church regarding how we take part in this memorial feast we refer to as the Lord's Supper, or Communion. He challenges us to examine ourselves for two things: making sure we are in the faith and confessing all that is in us that does not please the Savior.

This is the mood in which He established His feast in Matthew 26, and it should be the tone of our own hearts when we partake of His table. Out of the ancient rite of Passover, Jesus, in simplicity, lifts two elements of the feast from which to create His memorial.

Bread: "While they were eating, Jesus took some bread, and after a blessing, He broke it and gave it to the disciples" (v. 26). Though this bread pictured the suffering He would endure on our behalf, He gave thanks for it! Yet it pictures for us not only His suffering but His continuing provision for us as well. He is the "Bread of Life" (John 6), and Jesus pictured that marvelous reality with a symbol designed for us to take in, to taste, to experience in the most personal of ways. Imagine the sober quietness and the haunting silence of the upper room as the disciples watched Jesus break the bread, telling them to eat and saying, "This is My body" (v. 26). They must have wondered at those words as they took and ate.

Cup: Again, in spite of what it pictured—His blood offered as the sacrifice to cleanse us from sin—Jesus gave thanks (vv. 27–28)! The wine symbolized something deeper, however. It pictured the blood of the Passover Lamb that would end the slaughter of Passover lambs forever. It was specifically called the Cup of Redemption and was connected to the third of the great promises of Exodus 6:6–7: "I will redeem you." And that is precisely what the shedding of Christ's blood would accomplish—redemption. His blood would remove sin, resolve guilt, and exhaust the eternal penalty of sin. As the Eleven partook of it with thankful, awestruck hearts, so should we whenever we participate in His table.

They have already had a long, emotional, and stressful evening, but the night has just begun. The feast is adjourned, and the group leaves the upper room—without drinking the fourth and final cup of the unconcluded, yet now finished, Passover celebration. The fourth cup is linked to the kingdom, which explains Christ's statement that He would not again drink of the fruit of the vine until the kingdom had come (v. 29). Every detail has been attended to and every issue resolved. Now, they depart into the night singing (v. 30) the traditional closing psalms of the Passover celebration, Psalms 115–18. By the reckoning of the Jewish calendar, where the new day begins at sundown, it is now already the day of the Cross—yet, as Jesus participates (along with His men) in these psalms of worship and praise, He sings, "This is the day which the LORD has made; Let us rejoice and be glad in it!" (Psalm 118:24). It is the day of the Cross—pictured in bread and wine. It is the day of suffering—memorialized in a celebration feast. It is the day that the Lord has made, and He rejoiced in that day—the day that would bring Him death, and the death that would bring us life.

I must confess that as that young boy in the balcony of our church so many years ago, I did not comprehend the significance of the Lord's Table. In fact, for years to come it just seemed to be (and was often treated as) a mechanical ritual that was generally tacked onto the end of the service. As I grew up and eventually embraced the cross symbolized in the Table, all of that changed. I find it extraordinarily difficult to approach the memorial feast with anything less than the sober reality of what my sin cost my Savior and the wonderful assurance of how deeply and profoundly God loves. A few thoughtful impressions from an upper room are helpful to remind us of both.

Living Christ, there is no altar on which to offer sacrifices and no need for them. The Table displays Your love, and the sacrifice of Your grace is pictured for our hearts to embrace. Thank You for Your sacrifice. Thank You for the Cross. Thank You for the crumbs of broken bread that remind us of Your sufficient supply and for the cup that reminds us forever that You have kept Your promise to redeem us. Remind us of our frailty and our dependence upon You. Help us to respond to Your unspeakable gift with worship, love, gratitude, and obedience—that our hearts may display the grace You have freely given. Amen.

TWO

ON THE ROAD TO GETHSEMANE

What in the world could J. R. R. Tolkien have in common with Bob Hope? On the surface, perhaps not much. But there was at least one insightful theme expressed in their work: Many times in life, the journey is just as significant as the destination.

During the 1940s, Bob Hope and Bing Crosby became Hollywood stars and internationally known entertainers through a series of films that have come to be known as the Road pictures. This series of films featured the antics of Hope and Crosby as they traveled to some exotic destination—beginning in 1940 with *The Road to Singapore.* Over the course of the next twenty years, their adventures took them to Morocco, Zanzibar, Utopia, Rio, and Bali. Their travels ended in 1962 with *The Road to Hong Kong,* but along the way their audiences were able to visit exotic and mysterious locales they could only dream of in a day when international travel was rare. The point of the movies was not only arriving at the destination, but also for audiences to watch (and laugh about) the fascinating things that happened to Bob and Bing during the trip—the lessons learned on the road.

Similarly, in Tolkien's classic fantasy trilogy, *The Lord of the Rings,* Frodo Baggins sets out with eight companions (the Fellowship of the Ring) to take the one ring of power to the fires of

Mordor to destroy it—and to save Middle Earth from destruction. Throughout the trilogy, the destination of Mordor is always in view. Lurking in the distance, it is the inescapable reality that awaits Frodo and his friend, Samwise Gamgee. Yet most of the story is not focused on Mordor. It is instead preoccupied with the events, relationships, and life-changing challenges that take place as the adventurers make their pilgrimage to a dark and deadly place—events that shape the character of the travelers and prepare them for the destination on the ever-closing horizon. The journey itself becomes the significance of the story, and depth and meaning are drawn from the trials, triumphs, and near-death incidents the characters experience—the lessons of the road.

We, too, are people of the journey. In his excellent book *A Long Obedience in the Same Direction*, Eugene Peterson cites Paul Tournier, who refers to this as the experience of being "in between." He says the journey is

> between the time we leave home and arrive at our destination; between the time we leave adolescence and arrive at adulthood; between the time that we leave doubt and arrive at faith. It is like the time when a trapeze artist lets go the bar and hangs in midair, ready to catch another support: it is a time of danger, of expectation, of uncertainty, of excitement, of extraordinary aliveness (p. 20).

This "journey" concept is familiar to followers of Christ for, to the believer, life is often as much about the journey as it is about the destination. The culture that has cut its teeth on the phrase "Are we there yet?" needs to embrace the value of the journey. To a people who routinely refer to much of the land area of America as "fly-over country" (not places to be seen, but simply to be transmigrated), it is important to reflect not only on the lessons learned after "getting there" but also on the lessons that are available to be learned as we are on the way.

In Bible times, this was the essence of discipleship. A prospective disciple would attach himself to a rabbi (some kind of traveling teacher) and would live alongside him, learning the lessons of life as they experienced it together—eating together, observing nature together, and, yes, walking together on the road of life. It was completely about the journey.

This was also the case in Christ's journey to the cross. The destination was the most dynamic, world-shaking event in human history, and it is appropriate to give that event serious attention. At the same time, there were important things that took place while Jesus and His men were "on the way"—not only through their ministry travels for some three years, but even in the moments following the supper as they were traveling from the upper room to the garden of Gethsemane. Important things happened on the road to Gethsemane, and we often do not adequately pay attention because we are so anxious to "survey the wondrous cross." Here, we want to give our attention to discovering what happened along the way—in particular, on the road to Gethsemane. This portion of the passion story is often neglected, yet it describes significant events. We tend to rush to the garden where He will be betrayed, but Jesus continued to teach and prepare His men, taking full advantage of one final opportunity to minister to His men "on the road."

THE SHEPHERD'S LOVE

As we have seen, the Passover feast, which Jesus had made His own memorial supper, ended with the singing of psalms. That feast had been punctuated by the profound teaching of the Savior that is often referred to as the Upper Room Discourse (John 13–16). This would constitute His final significant teaching time with the disciples, and the lessons are powerful—among them are the promise of the Father's house (14:1–4); the coming Holy Spirit (14:16–26); the vine and branches (15:1–11); and the reality of Christ's impending death and resurrection (16:16–22). What is often lost in the shuffle, however, is a point of movement. It is a moment of departure and reentry onto the road. Subtle, yet distinct, is the statement of Jesus to His men in John 14:31. After teaching them of His own journey back to the presence of the Father, Jesus says, "Get up, let us go from here."

His words are so delicately folded into His teaching that they are easily overlooked. Unquestionably, however, they are words that take Jesus and His men from the quiet seclusion they had enjoyed and put their freshly washed feet back on the road. He continues to teach them in John 15–16 and intercedes for them in John 17—all while they are making their way to the garden of betrayal. It is only when they arrive there in John 18 that His attention turns from them to the Father and the mission of rescue ahead. But on the road we see the heart of the Good, Great, and Chief Shepherd for His little flock. It is there that He warns them, encourages them, strengthens them, and prepares them for the horrors that will come in a matter of hours. It is late at night, the streets are dark and quiet, and their conversation is held in hushed tones. The road leads them through Jerusalem, outside the city gates, across the Brook Kidron, and to the garden, but it also leads Christ to the cross—and all this weighs on His words as He shares His deepest concerns with them.

Amazingly, after all that Jesus had been teaching them in the upper room and on the road, they struck a familiar and distressing chord. Once again, they began to debate among themselves who should have the chief place. Luke 22:24 records the discussions: "And there arose also a dispute among them as to which of them was regarded to be the greatest."

While Christ is focused on the cross, they see only a crown— *their* crown. In response to their self-promotional argument, Jesus added further insight to His coming suffering. The new information was that they—His own disciples—would contribute to His suffering by abandoning Him at the hour of crisis: "Then Jesus said to them, 'You will all fall away because of Me this night, for it is written, "I WILL STRIKE DOWN THE SHEPHERD, AND THE SHEEP OF THE FLOCK SHALL BE SCATTERED"'"(Matthew 26:31).

In this statement, Jesus affirmed the Old Testament predictions of His passion by citing Zechariah 13:7 and applying it to Himself. With the ammunition of Zechariah's prophecy, He made three important predictions:

- *all* the disciples will be "made to stumble"
- the Shepherd will be struck down
- the sheep of His flock will be scattered

In the midst of their personal power plays, these words had to have had a startling impact. To drive His point home, our Lord used a very descriptive word to describe their abandonment. It is the word *skandalon*, translated here as "made to stumble." In fact, this word means "to be offended." In 1 Corinthians 1:23 the word is translated *stumbling block,* and the word ultimately describes being ashamed of someone or something. Now, in the relative safety of a quiet night on a dark and abandoned road, they happily talk of kingdoms and crowns and power and glory. But when the critical moment comes, they will become ashamed to be identified with

Him—and will abandon Him! And though Peter will have his own set of issues to deal with this night, Jesus' words are comprehensive: All of them will be offended; all of them will stumble; all of them will be ashamed—"because of Me." It is Christ Himself that they will abandon, and, as a result, they will be scattered to wander without a Shepherd, without direction. The Shepherd (Christ Himself) will be taken, and they will all flee in that moment.

Their Response to the Coming Trial

They respond with outrage! Jesus says that all will flee, but they all protest (Matthew 26:35). In the end, however, when Roman troops and Jewish temple guards come to arrest Jesus, the disciples' response is for self-preservation. As the soldiers take Jesus, Matthew humbly records, "Then all the disciples left Him and fled" (26:56)—all, including Matthew himself. Jesus is warning them on the road that they are not ready for the pressure that awaits them. Why? Because they have already forgotten the self-doubt that they had felt in the upper room and have begun to pursue self-promotion again instead. They were setting themselves up for personal disaster because they were not prepared for the pressure of the moment to come. As a result they would fail the test. They are on the verge of becoming victims of a pressure for which they have not prepared.

Pressure is a powerful force that in nature can either crush stones or form diamonds. Under life's pressures, one person soars and another falters. In fact, I think you could build a pretty strong case that the mark of a greatness is not always found in the level of a person's talent, ability, or skill. The real mark of greatness is revealed in how a person responds under pressure. This was certainly true of Dan Marino during his record-breaking career as a quarterback in the National Football League. Scouts, opposing coaches and players, and fans alike marveled at Marino's ability to see the field, skill-fully read a defense, and, especially, quickly release when throwing a football. Yet none of those elements would have been useful to him had he not been able to stand in the pocket and patiently wait for the play to open up—seemingly oblivious to the onrushing three-hundred-pound defensive linemen! In the midst of a cauldron of energy and, at times, chaos, Marino gave the calm appearance of being in the eye of the storm, where all is still. In spite of the pressure of the game situation, he was under control—and many of the resulting records he set as a passer may never be broken.

Tragically, newspapers, internet articles, and police blotters are filled with examples of athletes who had immense physical ability yet nonetheless failed because they buckled under the pressure. Sometimes their response to the pressure was to turn to drugs or alcohol. Sometimes they responded with violence or anger, and sometimes even suicide. The fact is that the power of pressure is not limited to the lives of professional athletes. People in all walks of life live in a pressure cooker with the temperature and resulting pressure constantly increasing. Homes are often a powder keg waiting to be ignited. Offices, factories, and workplaces can be intense seedbeds of rivalry and competition as companies seek, in the least, survival and, at the most, success in a global business climate that is increasingly unpredictable. Students encounter a growing pressure to excel, because simply having a degree no longer guarantees them of a job after graduation. The higher the grades, the better the chances might be—and the more powerful the stress to achieve becomes.

I do not think it is an overstatement to say that the way a person responds to pressure is one of the most telling elements of life in the modern world. How we respond to pressure is a very revealing thing, not only in what it tells others about us but in what we learn about ourselves in those moments of intense struggle.

The lesson of pressure is one that the disciples will fail to pass. It is a powerful lesson, and for them it is best learned on the road— for, as a result of their failure under pressure, they will lose their way and, left to themselves, will have no means of finding it again.

His Response to the Coming Trial

By contrast, Jesus' response to what will occur in the garden of their destination could not be more different. Notice again His words in Matthew 26:31: "You will all fall away because of Me this night, for it is written, 'I WILL STRIKE DOWN THE SHEP-HERD, AND THE SHEEP OF THE FLOCK SHALL BE SCATTERED.'"

As Jesus quotes Zechariah, He is affirming the most significant of all realities—God is in control! Zechariah, speaking on behalf of God the Father, says, "I will strike." Jesus recognizes that their abandonment is not at the heart of His coming suffering, for it is the plan of the Father for redemption, a truth that is affirmed in Old and New Testament alike:

- My God, my God, why have *You forsaken* me? Far from my deliverance are the words of my groaning. O my God, I cry by day, but You do not answer; And by night, but I have no rest (Psalm 22:1–2, emphasis added).
- Surely our griefs He Himself bore, And our sorrows He carried; Yet we ourselves esteemed Him stricken, *Smitten of God*, and afflicted (Isaiah 53:4, emphasis added).
- All of us like sheep have gone astray, Each of us has turned to his own way; But *the LORD has caused* the iniquity of us all To fall on Him (Isaiah 53:6, emphasis added).

- He who *did not spare His own Son*, but delivered Him over for us all, how will He not also with Him freely give us all things? (Romans 8:32, emphasis added).

It is impossible to realize the depths of the anguish of Christ's heart, especially His knowledge that the Father's own hand would apply His coming sufferings. Yet through the events of His passion, Jesus submitted to this Father-inflicted suffering and did not shrink from it. His confident trust in the Father's plan allowed Him to embrace the journey of suffering, rejection, and spiritual pressure unlike anything we could ever imagine. His trust allowed Him to accept, while the disciples' self-seeking would cause them to stumble and flee—abandoning the Shepherd, and, by their abandonment, the road of obedience. A significant contrast indeed.

This is tough stuff. The road is not what we always expect and sometimes what we personally might never choose. We are not capable of handling it on our own. We do not have a compass or road map for this journey. We must have a Guide who knows the journey as well as the destination. And that Shepherd pursues us when we, as Robert Robinson wrote, are "prone to wander, Lord, I feel it, prone to leave the God I love," and restores us to His fold. It is this commitment of the Shepherd to His sheep that gives hope to the disciples as Christ's dark and despairing words are still ringing in their ears.

A PROMISED HOPE

Perhaps more than anything else, human beings crave hope. In the midst of struggles, we endure because we hope for a day that will be better. In the shadow of failure, we stand up and move forward because we hope that the lessons learned will help us in the next challenge we face. Rob a person of money, and he will find a way to earn more. Take away a person's health, and she will learn to cope with her disadvantages. But if all hope is removed, it becomes very hard to get out of bed in the morning. Hope makes life endurable because it keeps us looking to the future—and what we trust will be a brighter day.

This is significant here because Jesus has just informed His men that they will abandon Him to His enemies—and the coming cross. Left with only that, their spiritual failure, when it occurs, could be suffocating. Their collapse could be terminal. It is important that they maintain a hope that stretches beyond the events of the next few hours. It is vital that they see the big picture—and the hope that is inherent in it. For this reason, the Master does not leave them with words of failure and despair. He adds to them words of hope. Notice: "But after I have been raised, I will go ahead of you to Galilee" (Matthew 26:32).

In spite of their coming desertion, Jesus gives them room for hope! All will flee, all protest Jesus' prophecy, and eventually all do run away, but all will be reunited! Even before they fail, Christ reassures them of restoration to Him and His presence. Not only does He offer them hope of reunion, He offers them the hope of the resurrection. All this will happen "After [He has] been raised." The root of all hope for believers is grounded in His resurrection from the dead. This is the testimony of the Bible to us: "Blessed be the God and Father of our Lord Jesus Christ, who according to His great mercy has caused us to be born again to a living *hope* through the resurrection of Jesus Christ from the dead" (1 Peter 1:3, emphasis added).

Hope is more than an optimistic perspective or a cheery outlook. Hope is a vital and vibrant confidence in the power of God to give life that lasts forever—a hope that is secured and validated by the resurrection of Christ Himself, the firstfruit of the resurrection (1 Corinthians 15). That is what makes this so important. Jesus doesn't tell them to shake it off or to keep their chin up or to not sweat it. He instead offers them substantial and significant hope—confidence that God will bring them restoration of heart and mind when Christ is raised from the dead.

So, what happened? Were the disciples encouraged by this? Sadly, no. Apparently, they never even heard what Jesus said because they were so consumed by His words of their coming failure! All that Jesus has warned them of will occur, but they will spend three days in utter despondency because they fail to consider the promise of reunion that Jesus gave them. Even facing the pressure of failure, the Eleven had the promise of restoration to Christ. They had been given the hope of renewed relationship with the God of all comfort. They had been warned of coming problems and confident solutions. Yet, in it all, they failed to embrace hope—and that failure, a step toward other failures to come, took an already dark night and made it even more distressing.

A SIFTED FAITH

In recent years, I have become increasingly disappointed in our process of selecting public officials. Since the 1980s, it would appear that elections and even appointments of significant governmental roles have become more and more destructive in both method and tone. In fact, it makes me wonder why a person would even want to run for office or accept an appointment to a position of leadership.

The only certainty in the process seems to be a thoroughgoing dismantling of the candidate's character, reputation, and family. Every instant of his life will be meticulously scrutinized. Every casual word or unthinking choice will be made the definition of her true self. Every failing and weakness will be exposed—and then attacked. If there is no indication of actual facts to expose concerns about the person's character, innuendo can be created to fill in the blanks. In a society where perception is reality, all that is needed is to create a shadow of doubt—whether it is reasonable or not—and our imaginations do the rest. The result is a public relations meat grinder that takes no prisoners and shows no mercy. It is a bloody and brutal process, and it is the essence of being publicly "sifted" in the modern world.

In the ancient world, sifting was the process of separating the wheat from the chaff. Now the process becomes a metaphor for spiritual testing, and as Jesus and His men inch ever closer to Gethsemane, He needs to warn Peter of this very thing. All the disciples will be ashamed. All will abandon Christ and flee. All will fail. But Peter will be sifted. It is the price he will pay for leadership, and it is the price he will pay for his boasts of trustworthiness—boasts he will not be able to live up to. It will be a time of testing that will rip any and all self-sufficiency from Peter and leave him broken. To see Jesus' warning most clearly, it is useful to switch to Luke's account, as he adds details not found in Matthew's record. (Note: Although Luke's record in chapter 22 appears to place this discussion in the upper room, Matthew's record, most noted for its careful chronology, places it on the road to the garden. Compare Luke 22:39 to Matthew 26:30.) Here, we will base our discussion on Luke 22:31–34.

The Source of Peter's Sifting

Simon, Simon, behold, Satan has demanded permission to sift you like wheat (v. 31).

In Matthew 16, Jesus had renamed this disciple Peter, the rock, but now He refers to him as Simon—his old name—as a warning that he is in danger of returning to his old ways! Then Jesus repeats that name in order to get Simon's attention. He must hear the warning if he is to be prepared for what is ahead. The warning? The Enemy has his sights set on you, Peter!

This is the nature of Satan, our spiritual adversary. He has one desire for believers, and that is to uproot their faith. He may seek to do so in a variety of ways—guilt, failure, shame, despair, temptation—but his goal remains the same. Derail the believer and nullify any effectiveness that he or she might have. This is the essence of the Enemy's attack, and it is as destructive as it is subtle. Yet, Satan is what he is. He is described in the following ways:

An accuser: "Then I heard a loud voice in heaven, saying, 'Now the salvation, and the power, and the kingdom of our God and the authority of His Christ have come, for *the accuser of our brethren* has been thrown down, *he who accuses them* before our God day and night'" (Revelation 12:10, emphasis added).

A roaring lion: "Be of sober spirit, be on the alert. Your adversary, the devil, *prowls around like a roaring lion*, seeking someone to devour" (1 Peter 5:8, emphasis added).

A destroyer: "But put forth Your hand now and touch all that he has; *he will surely curse You* to Your face" (Job 1:11, emphasis added).

Here, Peter's experience will mirror Job's in the Old Testament. In Job 1:8, we read of a dialogue in the heavens where God questions Satan. "The LORD said to Satan, 'Have you considered My servant Job? For there is no one like him on the earth, a blameless and upright man, fearing God and turning away from evil.'" The word *considered* is very important. It means, "to watch with evil in your heart." In today's parlance, God is asking Satan if he has been stalking Job with malicious intent. Satan had been studying Job, looking for a weakness—for a chink in the armor, for a soft spot that he could exploit.

Apparently, the same was true for Peter. Satan, the "roaring lion," had been stalking Peter's life, looking for his spiritual vulnerabilities in order to destroy him—and he had found them. The result is one of the most fascinating elements of this passage. Having considered Peter's weaknesses and developed a strategy, Satan went to God and "demanded permission to sift" Peter—and God granted him that permission! Now Peter will endure the most painful days of his life as he is sifted like wheat. As he enters this episode of spiritual and emotional agony, however, there are two things that he will need to remember:

1. Satan can't sift a believer without getting God's permission to do so. The Father is still in control, even in those moments when the pain and heartache of life feel out of control. He needs to keep his focus squarely on God—not on the trial or the Enemy.
2. Satan may sift to destroy the wheat, but God allows the sifting in order to rid us of the chaff in our lives. What Satan intends for evil, God intends for good. What Satan seeks to do to bring harm, God uses to produce purity.

In 1 Corinthians 10:13, the "siftings" are referred to as "testings" and are seen as an inevitable part of life. Paul wrote, "No temptation has overtaken you but such as is common to man; and *God is faithful*, who will *not allow you to be tempted beyond what you are able*, but with the temptation will provide the *way of escape* also, so that you will be able to endure it" (emphasis added). His message to us? This is life in a fallen world—but God is faithful. He can be trusted. He can be relied upon. He will not fail us, no matter how seriously we might fail Him. And because God is faithful, He provides a way of escape. What is it? I think Jesus' words to Peter have the answer.

The Root of Peter's Security

"But I have prayed for you, that your faith may not fail; and you, when once you have turned again, strengthen your brothers" (Luke 22:32).

Satan may petition God out of a desire to destroy, but Jesus petitions the Father in order to defend! What amazing words the Savior offers to the troubled disciple—"I have prayed for you." This is the mystery of grace, for Satan's sifting is overwhelmed by Christ's intercession. The power of this for us is found in the fact that He is our intercessor as well. The writer of the letter to the Hebrews affirms this: "Therefore He is able also to save forever those who draw near to God through Him, since He always lives to make intercession for them" (Hebrews 7:25).

The risen Christ always lives to intercede on our behalf! Yet in Peter's case, it is not only important to see *that* Jesus prays for us, we must also consider *how* Jesus prays for us. In Luke 22:32, our Lord does not pray to remove the coming trials, does not pray for Peter to have extra strength to face the trial, and does not pray that Simon Peter will be able to understand the reason for the suffering to come. Jesus simply prayed that Simon's faith would not fail. His faith—why?

• It is the shield of faith that defends us from the flaming arrows of the wicked one (Ephesians 6:16).

• Our ultimate spiritual security is rooted in Christ's work on our behalf—not on our ability to endure!

The impact of all this would be seen in the coming hours. Peter's love would fail, as would his strength, courage, and commitment. But his faith did not. Even in his cowardly denials, Peter never stopped believing in the Christ. This places a mile marker on the journey for us as well. We must never allow the pains and disappointments of life to cause us to lose sight of the fact that there is an Advocate at the right hand of the Father, always interceding on our behalf! He is there for us, as John writes, "My little children, I am writing these things to you so that you may not sin. And if anyone sins, we have an Advocate with the Father, Jesus Christ the righteous" (1 John 2:1).

He tests, protects, and prays for His child that the chaff might be sifted from our lives and that the true wheat of our hearts would be enduring faith. How would Peter respond to this warning and Christ's promise of intercession?

The Sadness of Peter's Response

But he said to Him, "Lord, with You I am ready to go both to prison and to death!" (Luke 22:33).

But Peter said to Him, "Even though all may fall away because of You, I will never fall away."

> *Jesus said to him, "Truly I say to you that this very night,*
> *before a rooster crows, you will deny Me three times."*
> *Peter said to Him, "Even if I have to die with You, I will*
> *not deny You." All the disciples said the same thing too (Mat-*
> *thew 26:33–35).*

Combining Luke's record with Matthew's, we see the sad result. The self-doubt seen in the upper room is now long gone, replaced by arrogant bravado. This self-confidence will be Peter's undoing as he offers three responses to the special warning of the Savior.

- **Disbelief:** "Not me!" In effect, Peter says to Christ, "Sorry, Lord, but you have this thing all wrong. I'm Peter, remember me? How could you even imagine that I would turn on you and abandon you? Don't worry about me, Jesus—I can handle it!"
- **Denial:** Here, Peter's argument gets really personal. It is as if he points to the other disciples and announces, "These guys are the ones you need to worry about! They have seemed just a little too weak all along. They may fall away from you, but don't worry about it. You can depend on me. I am there for you, Lord!"
- **Death rather than desertion:** His final words show the extent of his self-sufficient mindset. "Tough times are coming, you say? Maybe prison? Maybe death? I don't sweat that. I signed on for the long haul. I will be with you all the way to the finish line, Lord. Count on it!"

Before we are too tough on Simon, we need to see that his responses reflect his genuine love for Christ. He truly loves the

Lord, but it is a love that is a little too superficial and more dependent upon self-reliance than it is dependent upon the Master. In fact, perhaps what Simon Peter is most in need of understanding is that these are the very attitudes that cause him to need this sifting in the first place. He must learn to rely on Christ instead of self. He needs to recognize the value of the intercessions of Christ over his own frail flesh. Instead, Peter's self-reliance will result that night in three separate denials that he even knows the Christ he has just promised to die for.

To help Peter process what is ahead, once again Christ reaches out in compassion with a personal promise: "And you, when once you have turned again, strengthen your brothers" (Luke 22:32).

Peter will fail, but Jesus affirms that He is not yet finished with this fisherman. There will be a restoration, and there will be an ongoing service to Christ—but it will no longer be rooted in dependence upon self. It will be the painful lesson of dependence upon Christ that will equip and enable Simon Peter to lead the apostolic band and bring glory to Christ. As they approach Gethsemane, it has not been a particularly long journey (perhaps no more than one to one-and-a-half miles), but it has been a very revealing one. The lessons of the road carry a sting—and a shock. But the lessons are necessary, for a night of great darkness awaits them.

Through all the events of this dark road, we see Jesus Christ. We see Him as the great Prophet, declaring to His men needful truth. We see Him as the great Sufferer, grieving over our sins and failures and pride. We see Him as the great Advocate, interceding for His own. We see Him as the great Savior, redeeming even those who sometimes stumble and fall and deny Him. He has warned, and they have loudly protested. He has promised, and they have turned a deaf ear.

Now they draw ever closer to the garden—and perhaps the single most poignant element of the suffering of Christ. But along the way we have seen these truths:

- Satan and his limited ability
- Peter and his desperate need for sifting
- Ourselves and our need for spiritual dependence upon Christ

But most of all, we see Jesus and His wonderful grace as He cares for us, prays for us, and works in our lives—even in our pain, even in our sifting, even in our failures. So the questions presented to the Eleven now come to us.

- Am I in the sifting process? If so, I can't try to resist in my own strength. I must rest in Him and in the Father.
- Am I in the healing process? If so, I need to submit to Christ and let Him use my pain to strengthen others.

Yet regardless of where you or I may be in the process, it is vital for us to see the compassion of Christ, who never stops caring for us—even when we are in the sifter. That is why the hymn writer wrote words that form a prayer of comfort:

I must tell Jesus all of my trials;
I cannot bear these burdens alone;
In my distress He kindly will help me;
He ever loves and cares for His own.

I must tell Jesus all of my troubles;
He is a kind, compassionate Friend;
If I but ask Him, He will deliver,
Make of my troubles quickly an end.

Tempted and tried I need a great Savior,
One who can help my burdens to bear;
I must tell Jesus, I must tell Jesus;
He all my cares and sorrows will share.

I must tell Jesus! I must tell Jesus!
I cannot bear my burdens alone;
I must tell Jesus! I must tell Jesus!
Jesus can help me, Jesus alone.

THREE

ALONE IN THE GARDEN

Holy place is an interesting term. It invokes thoughts of quiet meditation, reverent worship, and soft prayers. Yet most of the sites that are considered holy places are much more tied to religious tradition than to actual holiness. In Israel, many places are referred to as holy because they are identified with a particular faith community—places like the Olivet Russian Orthodox Church or the Al Aqsa Mosque on the Temple Mount or the Western (Wailing) Wall, which represents the last remaining portion of Herod's first-century temple. A visit to the wall requires certain protocols and certain types of behavior, for to those of the Jewish faith, the Temple Mount is their highest holy site.

I think, however, that a true sense of the term *holy* is much more appropriate when it takes into account more than simply a location in time and space. At the side of a dying believer as she is leaving this life and entering the presence of Christ—that is a holy place. In the presence of a person in the moment he humbles his heart and embraces Christ as his own personal Lord and Savior— that is a holy place. Holiness is not an issue of religious rites or ecclesiastical atmosphere. It is that magnificent instant when the temporal and the eternal intersect in time and space. A place or time is made holy when God engages Himself in our most significant life events.

Perhaps no other place has that sense of wonder and holy awe been more thoroughly present than in the garden of Gethsemane. It is here that Christ wrestled with the cross and the will of the Father—and it is here that He embraced both in order to secure our rescue from a judgment we rightly deserve. As one man said, it is here that, like Moses, we feel compelled to take our shoes off of our feet, for in the Gethsemane experience of the Savior, we are truly on holy ground. Of this holy place and what would transpire there, F. L. Knowles, cited in Hendrickson's commentary on the gospel of Mark, writes, "Joy is a partnership, Grief weeps alone, Many guests had Cana, Gethsemane but One."

In his commentary on Matthew, William Hendrickson himself adds,

> Never shall we . . . be able to grasp how the human nature of Christ, in these solemn moments, related itself toward the divine, and vice versa. To the intense sufferings, experienced in Christ's human nature, was given infinite value by means of the union of this human to the divine nature, within the second person of the Holy Trinity.

It is in the holy place of the Scriptures that we come with hushed hearts and wide eyes to watch the anguish of the God-man as He embraces the cup of suffering for which He had come into the world. It all happens in the darkness of a garden.

A GARDEN SANCTUARY

When Jesus had spoken these words, He went forth with His disciples over the ravine of the Kidron, where there was a garden, in which He entered with His disciples (John 18:1).

It is now deep in the night. After the supper and the long walk to the garden, during which Jesus has warned His men and prayed to His Father, at last they reach the Brook Kidron, which ran outside the city walls. Kidron also served as a drainage run-off for the Temple Mount area, so it is likely that as the Lamb of God stepped across the stream, it would have flowed red with the blood of the thousands of Passover lambs that had been offered at the temple earlier that day—lambs that would never need to be offered again.

Jesus and His men cross the brook and make their way to Gethsemane—a significant place. Barclay described it well in his commentary on the gospel of John:

> Having crossed the channel of the Kedron, they came to the Mount of Olives. On its slopes lay the little garden of Gethsemane, which means the oil-press where the oil was extracted from the olives that grew on the hill. Many well-to-do people had their private gardens there . . . So to this garden Jesus went. Some wealthy citizen—an anonymous friend of Jesus whose name will never be known— must have given him the key to the gate and the right to use it when he was in Jerusalem. Often Jesus and his disciples had gone there for peace and quiet.

On a visit to Tabgha, in the Galilee region of the Bible lands, our group stopped at a site where the workings of an oil press were demonstrated for us. It was fascinating. There was a stone basin in which the olives were piled, and a large circular millstone, powered by a small donkey, which turned the stone until two things had occurred: all the olives were crushed beyond recognition and the life-refreshing oil had been drained from them for use. When the crushing stone was removed, all that remained was the shattered fruit.

That would be the experience of Christ in Gethsemane. In the basin of anguish and agony, He would be crushed and drained and used up—even before the cross had occurred. We need to enter the garden and observe—but I must confess to you that I do not fully grasp the depth of what is before us. Here, as in the wilderness, the Savior faces the Tempter and a fierce battle is engaged, one that we view with a sad mixture of humility and horror. Here we stand in awe and worship and see what the Son of God endured there on our behalf. One of the early church fathers, Gregory, says of Christ's time in the sanctuary of the oil press: "I love God because I know Him. I adore Him because I cannot comprehend Him. So, I stand at the edge of the garden and worship Him—without all the answers."

AN HOUR OF PREPARATION

And He came out and proceeded as was His custom to the Mount of Olives; and the disciples also followed Him. When He arrived at the place, He said to them, "Pray that you may not enter into temptation" (Luke 22:39–40).

I firmly believe that there is no substitute for careful and thorough preparation. Because I was involved in developing a series of motor racing-related evangelistic materials, I had the opportunity to spend some time in two car shops for NASCAR racing teams. I have to confess that I was really intrigued by it all—and became a fan.

At Robert Yates Racing, we toured the shop—which was thousands of square feet large. The floor was clean enough to do surgery on, and the parts department had everything imaginable. Cars were being trimmed out for upcoming races, taking in consideration the conditions of the track in an attempt to achieve optimum performance. Meanwhile, the engine shop was revving new test engines that would give the cars the maximum amount of horsepower while staying—barely—within the rules. At the same time, the "over-the-wall" pit crew was in a different place practicing pit road stops that require the precision and choreography of the Moscow Ballet. I was astounded by the effort and expense involved in what amounted to one thing and one thing only—preparation.

The problem with preparation is that it isn't fun. I would much rather play nine holes of golf than hit balls on the practice range (and my scores show it). Tiger Woods and Ernie Els know that it takes a lot of work to make things look effortless. Without preparation, we are not, well, prepared. We have to invest the time and energy into that preparation if we are to be ready when the moment of opportunity arises. Whether in sports or in life, preparation is huge. The Boy Scout motto is right when it urges us to be prepared. There is no substitute for being ready, as any astronaut, surgeon, building contractor, or logistics specialist will tell you.

In the spiritual realm there is also much to be said for preparation. It brings us to a point of readiness where we, in the strength of Christ, are able to respond to opportunity, resist temptation, and make decisions that are rooted in wisdom. That night, as the disciples entered the quietness of Gethsemane, they were in desperate need of all the above—and for them the garden was intended to be a place for preparation.

As Jesus pushes into the seclusion of the garden, He takes with Him the inner circle of disciples—Peter and the sons of Zebedee (James and John, also called the "Sons of Thunder"). They had been privileged to witness the raising of Jairus's daughter from the dead (Mark 5:35–43) and the magnificence of the transfiguration of the Christ (Matthew 17:1–9). Now they would have the incomparable privilege of witnessing the beginning of sufferings—the agony of the oil press. Why did Jesus want them to see the suffering He would endure there? How would they benefit from seeing the Savior in the depths of grief and mourning? At least two reasons, I think, explain this moment:

1. **They had declared themselves to be worthy!** Peter (Mark 14:29, 31) had said he would not desert the Lord, and James and John (Mark 10:38–40) had said that they were able to take the cup that awaited Christ! They had no idea what they were saying—their glib self-confidence had placed them in significant spiritual jeopardy. These three brash, self-confident disciples who felt bullet proof needed to see His anguish so that they would see the need to be prepared for their own.

2. **They needed to prepare themselves for the dark days ahead while there was still time.** "Pray, so that you won't succumb to the temptation to come" was His warning to them. We need to listen carefully to that warning as well. Prayer reminds us how weak we are and how strong He is. Prayer prepares us for the spiritual challenges that come along with living in a fallen world. Prayer is the capstone of the whole armor of God that equips us for the moments, hours, and days that will overwhelm—the events that otherwise, if lived in the pitiful vulnerability of our own capacities, will break us down (Ephesians 6:18). You need to prepare for spiritual battle in the quietness of prayer, or you will collapse in the conflict. Peter, having failed to

take the opportunity to prepare, will suffer such a collapse in a matter of mere hours.

Jesus warned them, and we should listen. The hour of difficulty is almost always unexpected. You cannot always expect the unexpected, but you can prepare by preparing—you prepare in prayer. And this is where the shoe pinches, because prayer is often not easy, simple, or quick. The price is too high, the concerns we face too great, the consequences too far reaching. When prayer is addressing life-and-death issues, it is demanding, prolonged, and hard.

For these disciples, however, it has been a long day. They are weary of the events of an emotional week. They value the comfort of sleep more than the deliberate perseverance of prayer. And when they awake, the time of testing will be upon them—and they will be unprepared for it. Peter will not stand as he had promised, but will fall. James and John will not take the cup as they had promised, but will flee. The rest of the Eleven, as Jesus predicted, will be scattered like sheep without a shepherd. And the cause of these failures, humanly speaking, is a lack of preparation.

AN HOUR OF AGONY

Often words by themselves are very inadequate tools. Email is a wonderful thing, but it can sometimes confuse communication instead of clarifying it. Sometimes it isn't enough to send a note or drop a line. You simply need to sit down in the same room at the same table with a couple of cups of coffee and look each other in the eye. You have to be there. Words alone cannot adequately convey the sense of the moment.

I feel that frustration deeply as we move with Christ through His garden experience and attempt to describe it with words. Words seem inadequate to carry the weight of the moment or express the depth of His emotions. The garden is an experience unlike any other—it is the deepest form of spiritual agony intensified by Christ's deity.

Agony of Soul

And He took with Him Peter and James and John, and began to be very distressed and troubled. And He said to them, "My soul is deeply grieved to the point of death; remain here and keep watch" (Mark 14:33–34).

Luke, the physician, describes Christ's experience in terms that shock us. In Luke 22:44 he says Christ is in "agony," a word used to describe wrestlers engaged in a mighty struggle. And part of that mighty struggle is accentuated by the sense of isolation Jesus feels. His family had turned from Him (Mark 3:21ff.), the crowds had walked away (John 6:66), the Twelve had become Eleven, the Eleven were reduced to Three—and they were asleep. Utter aloneness and utter agony await Christ in the garden, the basin of the oil press. A hymn writer described it this way:

It was alone the Savior prayed
In dark Gethsemane;
Alone He drained the bitter cup
And suffered there for me.
Alone, alone, He bore it all alone;
He gave Himself to save His own,
He suffered, bled and died alone, alone.

The isolation. The temptation. The horrors of this night surpass descriptive terms. What Luke summarized in one word ("agony"), Mark described more fully, perhaps because he may have been an eyewitness. Notice the terms used in Mark 14:

- *"very distressed" (v. 33)*—The King James Version puts it "sore amazed." These words describe a state of terrified surprise.
- *"troubled" (v. 33)*—This conveys deep anguish and grief for which there is no point of relief.
- *"grieved to the point of death" (v. 34)*—It is as if Jesus is saying to them, "The burden I bear is crushing the very life out of me!"

Matthew 26:37 adds terms that refer to being terrified and disoriented—difficult concepts to reconcile with the omniscience of the Christ! Sheer terror strikes His soul for the very first time. The reality of unbridled evil—anticipated from all eternity past— is now faced head on. Yet what constitutes the horror Christ faces is not the physical anguish and torture that await Him in the brutality of soldiers, nails, and a cross, terrible though that will be. It seems that what overwhelms Christ is the weight of sin—the curse and the cup. The coming act of sin-bearing brings horror to His absolutely pure and sinless heart. No normal fallen person, bound by a sin nature and sinful choices, can fully appreciate the conflict in the Lord Jesus Christ's soul as He wrestles with the burden of our sinful failings. He had never experienced even the slightest shadow of sin, and soon He would be enveloped by it. As Paul wrote: "He [God the Father] made Him [God the Son] who knew no sin to be sin on our behalf, so that we might become the righteousness of God in Him" (2 Corinthians 5:21).

Imagine, the sinless Son loaded down with sin. One sin would have been a brutal attack on His eternal purity—but the sins of the entire world from all the ages were extraordinary. Because of His deity, His foreknowledge of suffering, and His sensitivity to the Spirit, our Lord experiences anguish far deeper than we could ever know. In eternity past, as the "Lamb slain from the foundation of the world" (Revelation 13:8 KJV), Christ had accepted His role as the redeemer judicially. Now, in real-time experience, terror is the reality of what that acceptance fully meant. In his commentary on Matthew, John MacArthur says,

> It was not that He had never experienced grief or distress over sin and death and over the isolation from His heavenly Father they would bring. He had always known that He had come to the earth to suffer and die for the sins of the world. But the climax of His anguish now began to intensify as never before, as His becoming sin in our place and His consequent estrangement from God drew near. His very soul was repulsed by the encroachment of His sin bearing, not because of His taking upon Himself there the full magnitude and defilement of all man's iniquity. His agony over that prospect was beyond description or understanding.

This is what the writer of the book of Hebrews wants us to see when he writes: "In the days of His flesh, He offered up both prayers and supplications with loud crying and tears to the One able to save Him from death, and He was heard because of His piety. Although He was a Son, He learned obedience from the things which He suffered" (5:7–8).

It is difficult to find a passage of Scripture where we see the perfect, sinless humanity of Christ as clearly as we do in the garden. And in this oil press, He endures a second agony.

Agony in Prayer

And He went a little beyond them, and fell to the ground and began to pray that if it were possible, the hour might pass Him by. And He was saying, "Abba! Father! All things are possible for You; remove this cup from Me; yet not what I will, but what You will" (Mark 14:35–36).

It is a powerful and compelling scene, without question. As Mark described it, all the verbs are in the imperfect tense. Christ kept falling and praying, falling and praying—until He came to be completely on His face in the dirt, prostrate before the Father.

His prayer? "If it be possible." Was it possible? Yes, with the Father, "all things are possible," but that was not the Father's plan. The physical toll of the anguish is described medically by Luke (22:44), the physician-evangelist-historian, who described Christ's countenance as marred, not by delicate droplets, but by thick, clammy masses of bloody gore, pressed by inner agony through the skin and mixed with sweat, until it fell to the ground in the dust of the garden. The medical term for this is *hematidrosis,* a condition so severe that it sometimes results in retardation or death. But Luke says that an angel came (just as in Matthew 4, after the temptation that launched Jesus' earthly ministry) and strengthened Him so that He could continue on to His death. Though medical explanations help by giving us one small piece of the story, the hymn writer says it even better:

But none of the ransomed ever knew
How deep were the waters crossed;
Nor how dark was the night that the Lord passed through
Ere He found His sheep that was lost.

Hear His cry of pain in anticipation of the forsakenness He was to endure: *Abba,* the Aramaic equivalent of "Daddy"! "Daddy, take the cup away!" That was indeed the source and object of His agony—the cup! The cup anticipated the cross, and the content of that cup was the judgment required by a world's worth of sins. In a series of three seasons of prayer (Mark 14:35–42), Christ wrestles with the implications of the cup and accepts it along with all of those implications on our behalf.

In a clear picture of His humanity, He feels the awful burden of sin, and His holiness is repelled by it—but submits to it. Only Jesus experienced this—the Father that will never forsake His own makes that possible by being willing to forsake His Son. That forsaking began in the garden oil press and would continue until the Son declares from the cross, "It is finished." He accepts the cup of our sin and our suffering and presses it to His lips—and drinks it to the bitter dregs, as alluded to by the Old Testament prophets: "You have made Your people experience hardship; You have given us wine to drink that makes us stagger" (Psalm 60:3). "Rouse yourself! Rouse yourself! Arise, O Jerusalem, You who have drunk from the LORD's hand the cup of His anger; the chalice of reeling you have drained to the dregs"(Isaiah 51:17).

Notice, though, that there is no hesitation between the request and the submission! He gives Himself to the Father's purposes and will not be moved away from it. As Hendrickson observes in his commentary on Luke, "The main point to bear in mind is certainly this, that the anguish which brought about this phenomenon was 'for us.' It was an indication of the Savior's undying love for the poor lost sinners He had come to save."

This is the essence of what made Gethsemane so amazing. Here, Jesus chooses the cross. He chooses to be the Lamb. At Gethsemane, the victory of Calvary was secured because, though the holiness of Christ caused Him to shrink from the suffering to come, His will never ceased to be in complete submission to the Father's plan. The words of Christ's prayer are powerful because they can never be prayed glibly or casually. A commitment to the declaration "what You will" opens the door for our hearts to embrace His often surprising, sometimes unnerving, occasionally challenging, and eternally satisfying plan—but it can often bring immediate difficulty. For us as well as Christ, there can sometimes be a great cost attached to submitting to God's will.

AN HOUR OF SUBMISSION

Then He came to the disciples and said to them, "Are you still sleeping and resting? Behold, the hour is at hand and the Son of Man is being betrayed into the hands of sinners. Get up, let us be going; behold, the one who betrays Me is at hand!" (Matthew 26:45–46).

With the battle fought and the decision made, Christ rises from His spiritual battle with the Enemy of our souls. The Master steps forward from the holy place, having endured the agony of the oil press, and moves with the dignity of a king to accept the kiss that carries with it the cup. As Christ alerts His men that the time has come, His calm assurance stands in stark contrast to the experience of Gethsemane He has just endured. Yet, as always, the One who came to do the Father's will was at peace with that will—and was resolute in His commitment to do all that the Father required. Paul says,

> *Have this attitude in yourselves which was also in Christ Jesus, who, although He existed in the form of God, did not regard equality with God a thing to be grasped, but emptied Himself, taking the form of a bond-servant, and being made in the likeness of men. Being found in appearance as a man, He humbled Himself by becoming obedient to the point of death, even death on a cross (Philippians 2:5–8).*

"Obedient unto death, even the death of the cross." That obedience was finalized and embraced in the garden of the oil press. With the crushing of Jesus came the resolve of obedience, the mystery of the God-man, a concept far beyond the grasp of our human minds. The Christ in the garden—a sight that should stir our hearts and minds to devotion.

Like J. Vernon McGee in his commentary on Luke, all I can do is stand at the edge of the garden and worship and watch—without the answers: "Stand in the hush of Gethsemane and listen. Do you hear the sob of His soul? Do you hear the falling drops of blood? Look yonder, in the garden, by an olive tree, and see, bending low in agony and prayer—the Saviour, who took upon Himself your humanity and mine."

Blessed Father, how could You love me this much? How could Your love be so rich that it would suspend the judgment I deserved, placing it instead on Your Son? I thank You for Your love—help me to rejoice in it. I thank You for Your grace—assist me to bring honor to it. Thank You for Your Son's obedience—enable me to mirror it. Thank You for Your often-mysterious will— teach me to embrace it. Teach me to live a life that is a holy place for Your presence. For obedience that flows out of love and awe of the Christ, I pray. Amen.

PART TWO:

CONDEMNATION

FOUR

BETRAYED BY A FRIEND

In his commentary on the gospel of Matthew, Dr. Matthew Coder observes that a person might name his son Peter or Paul and his dog Nero or Caesar—but no one will name even a dog Judas. The name is synonymous with the worst form of treason, treachery, and personal betrayal. For centuries the name has stood for ugliness and ultimate evil. Perhaps the arch-villain of *Star Wars,* Darth Vader, with his commitment to the Dark Side, approaches the vileness of Judas. But even Vader eventually submits to the power of the Force and mends his evil ways—unlike Judas, who remains a traitor to Christ to the end.

In light of that, it is interesting that in recent years there appears to have been an almost orchestrated effort to exonerate Judas from any personal wrongdoing. In the movie *The Passover Plot,* it is the other disciples who are the real villains—foisting onto an unsuspecting world the false story of a resurrected Christ. In *Jesus Christ, Superstar,* Judas is the only clear-thinking character in the musical, and the story closes with Jesus dead—hanging on the cross. To a lesser degree, the epic television mini-series *Jesus of Nazareth* presents Judas as an unwilling victim of the political maneuverings of people with powerful agendas—on one side, the Zealots, who want Rome driven into the sea; and on the other side, the religious leaders wanting access to Jesus because they desire to entrap and destroy Him. Through books, movies, and other vehicles, Judas is increasingly presented as a sympathetic character—at the least deserving to be pitied, at most to be mildly distrusted. Some say Judas only wanted Jesus to confront the religious establishment. Some say that he was only trying to push Jesus to declare His kingship. Some even say that Judas is the real hero, because, of all the disciples, only Judas stood up for his own convictions. In any case, at worst, Judas was simply misguided—certainly not a traitorous scoundrel in a black hat deserving the scorn of centuries. It is amazing the portrait some have constructed of him—when they carefully omit key pieces of information and replace them with more positively cast assumptions and spin.

The truth is that the only record we have of Judas's activity is painfully clear in its description. The Bible tells us vital information that helps us understand Judas's character and possibly discern motives for his actions. Judas was a thief, a liar, and a person who rejected the greatest possible Light—Christ Himself—and sold his friend for the monetary equivalent of a mess of pottage. In fact, Judas and the Antichrist of the end times are the only two characters the Scriptures describe as being possessed by Satan himself (Luke 22:3). In the end, Judas defiled everything he touched, including his name. The name *Judas* means "praise," yet he has become the poster child of the worst form of treachery. His greeting ("Hail, Master"), a word of joy, becomes a bitter thing in his mouth. Usually a gesture of love, a kiss becomes an evil tool of betrayal when Judas performs it.

Yet before we become too self-righteous in "Judas-bashing," I feel compelled to say that, in many respects, *we* are Judas. To be sure, our betrayal generally takes a more subtle form and is usually unaccompanied by Judas's arrogance or boldness. But it bears the same tragic end in our hypocrisy, our selfishness, and our passion to control God rather than to be controlled by Him.

- I see Judas in my life when I say one thing and do another.
- I see Judas in my life when I try to manipulate God for my own ends.
- I see Judas in my life when I seek to barter and trade for the blessings of God.
- I see Judas in my life when, having been confronted by the truth of the Word of God, I remain stirred but not changed.

All too often, I am—we are—Judas, and, like his, our praise is turned into an ugly thing by our self-promoting desires. So here we are with the disciple we love to hate, willing to examine his deeds, but not as ready to connect the dots that lead from his life to our own motives and intentions. And we now enter the garden and stand in the shadows to watch a kiss of betrayal that would expose the darkness of Judas's soul—a kiss of betrayal that is far too easy for us to deliver as well.

CONFRONTATION IN THE
GARDEN SANCTUARY

It's fascinating how brave people feel when they are part of a crowd. A Michigan resident, I was amazed at how boldly Michigan State University students rioted and started fires in the city of Lansing several years ago in response to the basketball team's loss in the NCAA tournament. Individually, the students would likely never dare such acts, but the mood of the mob is a persuasive thing. It emboldens people to commit unthinkable behavior. Perhaps that is why the Sanhedrin didn't send Judas and a couple of temple guards—they sent a mob. This was going to be the first-century equivalent of a lynching, so a lynch mob was in order.

Unfortunately for those MSU students, the anonymity of being part of the mob was taken away as video cameras filmed the scene so that police could use the video from those cameras to identify—and punish—the wrongdoers. Likewise, the writers of the gospel records use their pens to break down the anonymity of that mob into identifiable characters and factions. Exposed to the light of day, these men who felt so strong and brave under the safety of the shroud of darkness are revealed for what they really are.

The Band

Now Judas also, who was betraying Him, knew the place, for Jesus had often met there with His disciples. Judas then, having received the Roman cohort and officers from the chief priests and the Pharisees, came there with lanterns and torches and weapons. So Jesus, knowing all the things that were coming upon Him, went forth and said to them, "Whom do you seek?" They answered Him, "Jesus the Nazarene." He said to them, "I am He." And Judas also, who was betraying Him, was standing with them. So when He said to them, "I am He," they drew back and fell to the ground. Therefore He again asked them, "Whom do you seek?" And they said, "Jesus the Nazarene." Jesus answered, "I told you that I am He; so if you seek Me, let these go their way," to fulfill the word which He spoke, "Of those whom You have given Me I lost not one" (John 18:2–9).

The mob that was dispatched to arrest Jesus was, at best, a mixed multitude. Present in the crowd were the betrayer, Judas, as well as factions from both the Roman contingent quartered in the Antonio Fortress in Jerusalem and the temple guards. What makes this crowd most impressive, however, is not its composition, but rather its size. In John 18:3, we are told it was a "cohort," which some historians say may have numbered as many as six hundred men! Add to that detachment of battle-hardened Roman soldiers a representation of temple guards, and you have a very substantial group. In Matthew 26:47, we read that they came with "swords and clubs." The group would likely have been divided by forces, with the Romans brandishing the swords and the temple guards following with clubs. Notice that John says this huge group was sent "from the chief priests," which speaks to two different issues of interest:

1. This reveals the sense of desperation the religious establishment felt over the threat posed by the Nazarene. For them to join arms with the hated Roman occupation forces is nothing short of astounding.
2. It also reveals the degree of their fear because of the power Jesus had displayed in His ministry. To send such a mob to arrest a single person, surrounded only by a handful of former fishermen (as opposed to trained guards or soldiers), may reveal the depth of their concern about their ability to control the worker of miracles.

As the crowd entered the garden of Gethsemane, one other thing is interesting. John says that they came with "lanterns and torches." Why would they need them? Passover always occurs during the full moon, meaning that there would have been ample light for the accomplishment of their mission. Perhaps they thought they would have to search every nook and cranny of the garden to find Him, expecting Christ to be hiding in the dark shadows of the olive trees. What a surprise it must have been when Jesus stepped forward to meet them and even initiated dialogue!

As the mob moves to meet Him, Jesus gives them one more display of His divine authority. When they ask Him if He is Jesus the Nazarene, He declares, "I Am!" (Some Bible translations record His response as "I am He," but the word "He" is not in the original). Jesus answers with the ancient name of God Himself, and when He declares His divine identity, the mob is driven backward and falls to the ground! This powerful expression of the Person they had come to arrest and control now reveals Himself as a Person outside the limits of their control.

In all of this, it must be recognized that Jesus is not a victim; He is the victor. He had laid the plans for this moment in eternity past, and even now He is in complete control of the situation. In fact, He displays His control in two different ways:

- He reveals the truth of the words He had said: "No one has taken it away from Me, but I lay it down on My own initiative. I have authority to lay it down, and I have authority to take it up again. This commandment I received from My Father" (John 10:18). They were not taking Him captive—He was presenting Himself as the necessary sacrifice that must be offered for the world's sins.
- He cares for the welfare of His disciples when He asks twice whom they seek. Both times they answer Jesus, and Christ, fully in charge of the moment, demands that the disciples be released.

What an amazing scene, as the one who is the target of this lynch mob intimidates the crowd and drives them back with the authority of the living Christ—then, as a lamb led to the slaughter

(Isaiah 53), yields to their arrest. It is in this moment that Judas Iscariot moves in to finalize the identification—and to earn his pathetic thirty pieces of silver.

The Betrayer

While He was still speaking, behold, Judas, one of the twelve, came up accompanied by a large crowd with swords and clubs, who came from the chief priests and elders of the people. Now he who was betraying Him gave them a sign, saying, "Whomever I kiss, He is the one; seize Him." Immediately Judas went to Jesus and said, "Hail, Rabbi!" and kissed Him (Matthew 26:47–49).

Notice how bluntly Matthew states it: "Judas, one of the twelve." Those are such cutting words. Judas was one of the Twelve, one of those with great privileges, great honors, and great opportunities. He had witnessed the greatest teaching, miracles, and compassion ever seen. He had participated in ministry in the name of Jesus and had been trained at the feet of the Master Himself! Yet at the end of the day, Judas relinquished it all. It seems unfathomable to us that Judas could make such a choice, but there he is, stepping forward to identify Christ for His attackers, His soon-to-be tormenters.

Judas's words are masked in hypocrisy as he says, "Hail, Rabbi." This was a common greeting that meant, "I'm so glad to see you!" It was the ultimate in two-faced deception, and he somehow—wrongly—thought that he could get away with it. He then leans forward and "kisses Him." The form of the Greek verb here is strong and emphatic. It means that Judas embraced Jesus and kept on kissing Him. The intensity of the word reveals that Judas did not just betray Jesus—he did so enthusiastically. It is a word that is filled with passion, and it is the same word used in these passages:

- the sinful woman who kisses the Lord's feet and anoints them with perfume in Luke 7:38
- the father embraces and kisses the prodigal son when he returns home in Luke 15:20
- the tender farewell between Paul and the elders from the church at Ephesus in Acts 20:37

Judas betrayed Jesus energetically, not passively. The key thing to consider here is that Judas had betrayed Jesus long before this dark night in the garden sanctuary. The act of the kiss is merely the expression of how terrible that betrayal was. In his book *Be Transformed*, Warren Wiersbe points out,

> A kiss was a sign of affection and devotion. Members of a family kissed each other in meeting and in parting, but Judas was not part of God's family. Disciples greeted a rabbi by kissing him; it was a sign of devotion and obedience. But Judas was not truly a disciple of Jesus Christ... It was bad enough to betray Christ, but to do it with a *kiss*, a sign of affection, is the basest treachery of all.

Judas, with arrogance and energy, repeatedly kisses Jesus on the face! In his heart, Judas believed he could kiss the God-man on the face in mockery and get away with it—but God is not mocked (Galatians 6:7). What thorough hardness of heart Judas displayed! He had heard the teaching, seen the miracles, been warned, and been knocked to the ground. So we must ask the question, "How many times does the God of heaven have to knock a man down to wake him up and get his attention?" And before I try to answer, I must remember how much of the time I am Judas. I must remember how often I am, as the hymn writer put it, "Prone to wander, Lord I feel it, prone to leave the God I love."

COMPASSION FOR THE HEARTS OF MEN

During one of my trips to Russia, I had the privilege of preaching for a Communion service in an evangelical church in Moscow. Before the service, I was introduced to a man called "John Smith," who found great humor in telling me that was the English equivalent of his Russian name. He was an older man with dark, sunken eyes and very shaky hands. I asked my translator if "John" had Parkinson's disease or some other kind of debilitating condition of the nervous system.

"No," she responded. "Under Communism John would go on the street corners and preach the gospel. Repeatedly the secret police (the KGB) would arrest him, take him to Lubyanka Prison, and beat him. When they released him, as soon as he had recovered from the beatings and abuse, he would go back to the street corner and resume his ministry. Finally, the KGB agents told him that they were tired of beating him, so unless he would commit to never again preaching the gospel publicly, they were going to execute him on the spot. John refused their offer—and they shot him in the head. The agents dragged John from the building and threw him into an alley to die. By a miracle of God's grace, John survived and resumed preaching—even sharing the love of Christ with the KGB agents who continued to try and thwart his efforts to bring people to the love of the Savior."

I looked at John and realized how deeply he must love Christ to be able to so completely follow the Master's example that he could genuinely and deeply love those who hated and abused him. It is the best personal example I know of to describe compassion, and the Lord Jesus modeled it as He confronted the lynch mob that invaded the garden where He prayed. His compassion extended to the lives of those present—*all* of those present.

Compassion to the Betrayer

And Jesus said to him, "Friend, do what you have come for."
Then they came and laid hands on Jesus and seized Him (Matthew 26:50).

Surprised? Surprised that Jesus cares for Judas even as he betrays Him? We shouldn't be. Second Peter 3:9 powerfully reminds us of the depths of God's compassion: "The Lord is not slow about His promise, as some count slowness, but is patient toward you, not wishing for any to perish but for all to come to repentance." Even Judas? Yes, even Judas! In Matthew 18:7, Jesus, apparently speaking of Judas, says, "For it is inevitable that stumbling blocks come; but woe to that man through whom the stumbling block comes!"

Jesus had warned Judas, and now He reaches out to him. He calls His betrayer *friend*. Traveling companion. Associate. David prophesied about Jesus' feelings at this moment when he wrote, "Even my close friend in whom I trusted, Who ate my bread, Has lifted up his heel against me" (Psalm 41:9). Jesus reached out to Judas in love and compassion and was heartbroken at the hardness of Judas's heart—a hardness even the compassion of Christ could not break through.

Jesus then asked the question, "Are you betraying the Son of Man with a kiss?" (Luke 22:48). These were cutting words intended to wound, but not to kill. To reveal, but not to reward in kind. Why would Jesus ask the question?

- to show Judas the depth of his heart of treachery
- to show Judas that He is not deceived by his warm words and gentle actions
- to show Judas his need for repentance
- to show Judas that His own heart had not changed, though the heart of the betrayer had

Jesus pleads with Judas to consider what he is doing—even for Judas it was not too late! "Judas, set aside your sin and deal with it!" That is the compassion of Christ. That is the wonder of a grace that is amazing. It is the challenge to the redeemed heart from the heart of the Redeemer:

"But I say to you, love your enemies and pray for those who persecute you, so that you may be sons of your Father who is in heaven; for He causes His sun to rise on the evil and the good, and sends rain on the righteous and the unrighteous. For if you love those who love you, what reward do you have?" (Matthew 5:44–46a).

Compassion to a Man of the Mob

And behold, one of those who were with Jesus reached and drew out his sword, and struck the slave of the high priest and cut off his ear (Matthew 26:51).

Now Peter steps in. I think some credit must be given to him, because on the road to Gethsemane, Peter had promised Jesus that he would be there for Him. He would even die with the Master if that were what was called for. Now he rises to Jesus' defense with a sword hidden beneath the folds of his robe. Of course, as one teacher said, it must be remembered that Peter was a fisherman, not a soldier or a gladiator. He was accustomed to having nets and oars in his hands—not a deadly weapon. He may have been trying to take off the head of Malchus (John 18:10), the servant of the high priest, but, swinging wildly, Peter connected only with the man's ear—lopping it off.

Now there is a serious problem! It appears that the mob may be needed after all, for the Nazarene's men are attacking the duly appointed posse! But Jesus intervenes, Luke tells us: "But Jesus answered and said, 'Stop! No more of this.' And He touched his ear and healed him" (Luke 22:51). Malchus could have bled to death, or at the very least been badly disfigured—but Jesus showed compassion to him and touched him and healed him. This healing presents again the authentic power of Christ, this time to come to the aid of an "enemy."

Try to put yourself in the place of Malchus. Imagine all that he has seen and experienced this night—he has heard the ravings of the priests, listened to the comments of the other guards and soldiers, and entered the garden with great apprehension. But now he has seen the majestic Christ in calm control in the face of the mob. He has seen the power of Christ in full view, and he has felt in personal healing the care and compassion of this Man he has been sent to help arrest. Talk about mixed emotions! How do you apprehend the one who has just been your deliverance? How do you arrest the one who has just healed you? I often wonder about Malchus—what became of him? What did he tell his wife when he got home that day? What a strange journey he was on. Did his heart revert to the anger of the lynch mob? Did he embrace the Savior who had healed him? I just wonder if we might see him in heaven.

Compassion to a Failing Disciple

In what way did Jesus show compassion to Peter? By healing Malchus! One of the charges against Christ was the crime of insurrection, and now Peter was an accessory to that crime by virtue of having attacked the emissary of the chief priest. In fact, Bible scholars speculate that if Jesus had not healed Malchus, there would have been four crosses on Golgotha the next day, with the fourth bearing Simon Peter to his death. Even as He was being arrested, Jesus was protecting His own.

Peter's act, however, was an act of fear—the fear of failure! Peter wanted so desperately to stand firm, to be brave. But he had not prepared in the garden and now would collapse under the weight of his own expectations. In fact, even with a bloody sword in his hand, Peter's spirit is willing, but his flesh is weak.

How he must have wished, at the moment of testing, that he had heeded the warning of the Master. He had not, and now this long, dark night of pain had begun with an ugly turn. For Simon Peter, it would only get worse. For the Christ, the shadow of the cross looms ever larger before Him.

CONFIDENCE IN THE FATHER'S PLAN

The pastor had given his very best, he believed, but had been dismissed nonetheless. His heart was broken, his family in turmoil, and his dream of ministry brought to a screeching halt by the request of the board that he resign—or be fired. As we talked, we discussed what had gone well and what had gone poorly. We worked through areas where he needed improvement and areas where he had a platform on which to build. It was an emotionally bloody time for this wounded shepherd who truly did not understand why he had just lost his job. The pain, the uncertainty, the insecurity, the deep sense of personal failure all balled up together inside him to create an ache that would not soon go away.

The young father stood in the neonatal intensive care unit and watched as his infant daughter—on a respirator—struggled to maintain breath. The respiratory condition had developed suddenly, and with frightening speed his baby girl was rushing toward death's door. He wept and wondered, and we talked about grace and mercy and the power of God.

The single mom was swallowed up in bills from a deadbeat dad/husband who had left for a younger woman—laughing that he was trading in his forty (year-old wife) for two twenties. As she looked at what she was earning at the job she had been forced to take in order to support her kids, the pressure seemed more than she could bear. She wondered how she would keep her little family together while she waited for a husband who had proven skillful at doing the wrong things decided whether in this case he would do the right thing.

All three of these hurting, suffering, anguished hearts had one thing in common. As we discussed their personal seasons of trials, they expressed absolute confidence that God knew what He was doing and would bring good out of these bad times—the Romans 8:28 worldview. They accepted the paradigm of a sovereign God who in the long run always brings His best to His child, though sometimes in the short run He allows them to experience deep waters. Confidence in a God we don't always understand is born from a willingness to trust His character, even when we can't necessarily grasp His doings.

No one so unbendingly trusted God the Father's plan than God the Son. He rested in that plan so completely that the writer of Hebrews challenges us to follow Christ's example by "fixing our eyes on Jesus, the author and perfecter of faith, who for the joy set before Him endured the cross, despising the shame, and has sat down at the right hand of the throne of God" (Hebrews 12:2). In the garden He has faced the shame and the cross and moved to it with resolve and a willing heart. His final words in Gethsemane before moving toward His continuing trials reflect that deep abiding confidence.

To Simon Peter

Then Jesus said to him, "Put your sword back into its place; for all those who take up the sword shall perish by the sword. Or do you think that I cannot appeal to My Father, and He will at once put at My disposal more than twelve legions of angels? How then will the Scriptures be fulfilled, which say that it must happen this way?" (Matthew 26:52–54).

Peter needed to understand that the Father's plan was trustworthy! The fisherman's sword was not necessary, nor could it prove effective. If Jesus needed protection, twelve legions of angels—72,000 heavenly warriors!—stood ready to respond to His call. No such relief was necessary, however. Jesus had not fallen into the hands of the men who had come to arrest Him. Rather, He had rested Himself in the gentle hands of His Father's divine purposes. The event in the garden was over, and the purposes of the heavenly Father would be accomplished—in spite of the spiritual Enemy, the hearts of evil men, or the efforts of a misguided disciple.

To the Crowd

At that time Jesus said to the crowds, "Have you come out with swords and clubs to arrest Me as you would against a robber?

Every day I used to sit in the temple teaching and you did not seize Me. But all this has taken place to fulfill the Scriptures of the prophets." Then all the disciples left Him and fled (Matthew 26:55–56).

Jesus then addresses the posse that has come to arrest Him by challenging the integrity of their actions! He points out that their deeds are cloaked in hidden agendas and sinister motives, which has become apparent in this secret, nighttime arrest. The arrest could easily have taken place in the broad daylight of the temple courts where Jesus had openly taught and ministered.

Yet this was not about their plan—it was about God's plan. This is why, in speaking to Peter and to the crowd, Jesus stresses the only thing that really mattered. "All this has taken place to fulfill the Scriptures"—the plan is being brought to its necessary completion. The promised strategy for redeeming a lost humanity is absolutely on schedule. The Scriptures were being fulfilled, and that was the issue most vitally important to the Savior. Ancient words spoken by sages and prophets, recorded on scrolls, events hoped for and waited upon for centuries—all are now being fulfilled in a moment of history. The Father's plan was the right plan, and the Son of God trusted it all the way to the cross and beyond. In the garden, He had settled His acceptance of the plan, and now He had verbally confirmed that acceptance. For Christ, it is now time to move on, for the next part of the perfect plan awaits.

Then all the disciples left Him and fled (Matthew 26:56).

At the moment in which Christ displayed His unwavering confidence in the Father's plan, the poor disciples showed how weak their own spiritual stamina was. As Jesus had warned, all of them abandoned Him to the angry mob—and ran away. All had been warned of this moment, and all had failed to prepare. Now all run away to hide. But in the end, all of these eleven disciples will be restored. As Adam had learned, the God of the garden is the God of grace. As Jonah learned, the God that is sovereign is also the God of the second chance. As the disciples will learn, though they abandoned Christ, He will never abandon them.

In our own moments of spiritual desertion, we would do well to remind ourselves of the safety of His presence and the wonders of forgiving grace. He is the loving Lord who forgives our destructive choices as we confess them to Him. He is the mighty God who accomplishes His good will in our lives as we yield to Him. He is the saving Shepherd who cares for His own and protects us—sometimes even from ourselves and the worst inclinations of our hearts.

In the darkness, we try to hide from Your gaze, Lord Jesus, but Your eyes clearly see. Expose our hearts when they move toward treachery and self-seeking. Strengthen our hearts when we need to stand strong, and remind us of the perfect peace that comes when we rest in the matchless purposes of the Father's plans. Remind us that we do not need the weapons of the world or even the armies of heaven to protect us—we need only the Shepherd's powerful care. Help us to trust You with all our hearts. Amen.

FIVE

DENIED BY A FRIEND

Friendship is a risky business. When we become friends with other people, we expose ourselves and become vulnerable in surprising ways. It is this vulnerability that separates real friendships from mere acquaintances. With an acquaintance, we have the option of holding another at arm's length. We don't have to "let someone in" if we aren't convinced that we really want him or her that close to our true hearts and true thoughts and true selves. Country artist Trisha Yearwood captures these relationship boundaries in song: "I've got a wall around me that you can't even see. [It'll] take a little time to get next to me."

That is the relative safety of engaging life at the level of acquaintance instead of at the depth of true friendship. It is when we decide to let down our defenses and allow someone to enter into our lives significantly that we become truly vulnerable. Perhaps that is why studies show that most people will have fewer than five significant friendships in their lifetime. We are just too afraid of what will happen if we become that vulnerable—afraid to be exposed to the potential hurt if the friendship crumbles.

I am pretty certain that I first met Tommy in the fifth grade, though I can't remember life as a child without his being part of it. Through junior high and high school, Tommy and I were as tight as two friends could be. We did everything together—from double dating to a really lame garage band we started together. Tommy and I were, in Forrest Gump's words, "like peas and carrots." We just fit together as friends and assumed it would always be that way. Our friendship endured growing pains, pirated girlfriends, academic competition, driver's training, and the ultimate failure of the aforementioned garage band. Our friendship even survived when he went away to college and I stayed at home to work. It was a true friendship that seemed like it could endure anything—except the theological debate that surprised us both.

I had gone to Bible college at age 21, while Tom (no longer Tommy, just as by then I was no longer Billy) went to seminary. It seemed like everything was safe and solid, until we got together on Christmas break. We got into a conversation that led to a discussion that led to a debate that led to an argument on an issue that seemed so important at the time—yet seems pretty peripheral now. In an instant, a friendship that had lasted for over a decade was crumbled in a heap on the floor. We both walked away mad, and I decided that pain of that kind was too high a price to pay for friendship. I wouldn't allow myself to become that vulnerable again.

I think about Tom and the deep sense of loss I felt when our childhood friendship collapsed and am thankful that the Savior understands. In fact, Hebrews 4:15 tells me that He is touched with the feelings of my pain because He has been there, done that. He understands the struggle of losing a significant friendship, because meaningful friendships that He had been vulnerable to had likewise gone south. He too knew what it was to experience that disappointment. Now I understand that at least fifty percent of the responsibility of my failed friendship with Tom was mine (perhaps much more than fifty percent) and that Christ never failed anyone in any measure in any relationship—but the pain is the same. And He understands. His closest associate, His lead disciple, His chosen colleague would deny even knowing who Jesus was. Simon Peter, Jesus' dear friend, would deny having any kind of relationship with the Savior—let alone a deep, personal, life-changing friendship.

A WORD OF CAUTION

As we have walked with Christ and His men through these experiences to this point, we have seen the passion of our Lord unfolding with almost painful clarity. We have traced His steps from the upper room to the agony of the garden to the betrayal by Judas, and the stage is being carefully set for that hour in which, through the cross, Jesus Christ will be glorified.

There is no question that, in it all, the focus is on the Savior. He is center stage. He is in the eye of the storm—a storm of conflict raging between heaven and hell. Yet in the midst of all of this, all four gospel writers pause to focus their attention on Simon Peter. He will behave more like Simon than like Peter (the "rock") and will fail his Friend. Though all the gospel writers tell of Peter's denials, in John's gospel we see the account of Peter's failure woven into the narrative of the trials of Jesus. It is as if the apostle were trying to tell us that it wasn't only Jesus but each of us (with Peter) who was actually on trial that day! In that sense, Peter truly is Everyman. As Jesus had warned him on the road to Gethsemane, Simon Peter, the fisherman of Capernaum, was going to be put to the test—sifted—and would fail. His experience becomes to us an object lesson. Peter becomes a living parable of self-destruction and the choices and tendencies that produce that self-destruction. It is a subtle pattern, but one that will grieve Peter to the very fabric of his soul. That is why it is important that we not be too tough on Peter—in fact, it might be very useful if we could see ourselves and our own capacity to fail in his failure.

A SERIES OF UNFORTUNATE EVENTS

So the Roman cohort and the commander and the officers of the Jews, arrested Jesus and bound Him, and led Him to Annas first; for he was father-in-law of Caiaphas, who was high priest that year. Now Caiaphas was the one who had advised the Jews that it was expedient for one man to die on behalf of the people. Simon Peter was following Jesus, and so was another disciple. Now that disciple was known to the high priest, and entered with Jesus into the court of the high priest, but Peter was standing at the door outside. So the other disciple, who was known to the high priest, went out and spoke to the doorkeeper, and brought Peter in . . . The high priest then questioned Jesus about His disciples, and about His teaching. Jesus answered him, "I have spoken openly to the world; I always taught in synagogues and in the temple, where all the Jews come together; and I spoke nothing in secret. Why do you question Me? Question those who have heard what I spoke to them; they know what I said" (John 18:12–16; 19–21).

During the Cuban Missile Crisis of October 1962, President John F. Kennedy spent much time considering the implications of a book he had recently read, *The Guns of August*, by Barbara Tuchman. In it, the author had scrutinized the events that had contributed to the start of World War I. The historian's conclusion was that the war had started as the result of a series of circumstances that, while appearing to be unconnected, converged to produce the "war to end all wars." Kennedy fretted over this as he watched the escalation of events between the White House and the Kremlin—concerned that a similar set of presumably unaffiliated triggers could launch the first global thermonuclear exchange between the world's superpowers. To find yourself on a collision course with self-destruction is tragic. To be on that path and not realize the forces at work to bring about that self-destruction is doubly tragic.

Peter is on just such a collision course. His problems and his vulnerability did not begin in the courtyard in front of a fire—they had begun hours earlier. Now Simon will reap the fruit of the seed he has been sowing. Notice how his situation has progressively worsened as this night has gone on:

- **Self-confidence:** Peter had expressed too much trust in himself on the road to Gethsemane when Jesus had warned him to prepare for this moment of testing. He declared, "Though all the rest will abandon you I will not! I will die for you!" Yet he was like one person's description of a famous athlete, "His mouth's writing checks his body can't cash." Peter trusted in himself far too much.

- **Carelessness:** Simon's peril had deepened in the garden when Jesus asked him and the other disciples to watch and pray, but they chose instead to sleep. Jesus challenged, "Simon, could you not watch with Me one hour?" He had carelessly let the opportunity to prepare slip away and would come to regret it.

- **Self-effort:** When the arrest had taken place, Peter sought to rescue Jesus by force with a sword and misguided bravado—and had to be rescued by Christ Himself.

Now Peter finds himself in the wrong place at the wrong time. That will become painfully clear in the things he sees and feels.

What Peter Felt

Fascinating, isn't it? Individually, none of these character flaws would seem to be overly grievous—but together they produce an increasingly combustible situation that will burn Simon down. Christ had specifically intervened in order to protect His little flock one last time, and Peter had rejected that protection—choosing instead to step away from the security of the Shepherd's defense and placing himself squarely in jeopardy.

Here we see the heart of Peter at war with itself. On the one hand, he truly loves Jesus and wants to keep his promises to the Master. On the other hand, however, is our fear and self-protection when our world starts to unravel like a cheap sweater and we feel powerless to stop the pain. The words of Christ in the garden were as prophetic as they were accurate: The spirit was willing, but the flesh was weak. Sending out a batch of mixed signals, Peter desperately wants to follow Jesus—but he does so at a distance, within the comparative safety of the crowd. He tries to blend in and make himself inconspicuous. He wants to be with Jesus and see what will happen but still not be close enough to be identified as one of the Master's men.

Peter is about to understand just how painfully easy it is to make promises and how difficult and costly it is to keep those promises. He must have felt the gravity of his failure in the garden, consummated with one ill-advised swing of his sword. Perhaps he felt nothing more than just a desire to be close to Christ. Regardless, whatever he felt, Peter didn't feel it strongly enough to declare his allegiance to the Teacher that had been arrested like a common criminal. In the end, Peter's fears overwhelmed his love. He stood by—but as John said, "from a distance."

What Peter Saw

You just can't prepare for some things in life . Things like holding your newborn child in your arms. Things like watching that child get married. Things like having that child give you a grandchild. You just can't prepare for the emotions that accompany these important events.

But there are other less positive situations that we face in life that we can't ever truly be ready for. Visiting a poverty-stricken and disease-laden village in Africa. Seeing the effects of a terrorist bomb on an Israeli commuter bus filled with ordinary people guilty of nothing more than getting up in the morning and going to work. Or, in Peter's case, seeing your dearest friend arrested on false charges, beaten mercilessly, and condemned to an undeserved death. Peter had been warned to prepare—but I suspect the events of that night were things for which he could have never been really prepared.

As Peter followed at a distance, the pathway of Christ's passion led to the home of the high priest, where the first round of trials would occur. As Peter watched, he saw things he was unprepared for. He saw the Savior being interrogated like a common thief. He saw Jesus being beaten and abused, both physically and verbally (Matthew 26:67–68). He looked on and listened as two witnesses, with contradictory testimony, lied about the One who is Truth. He watched as a charade of false justice began to weigh in against the Righteous Judge. This is what he saw.

But what Peter saw needs to be understood. Matthew 26 says that Peter came to "watch"—but he was not there to see miracles and healings or to hear the Master Teacher. He had not come to see deity on display. Peter had come to watch as a lamb—the Lamb of God—was led to the slaughter. He was witnessing the beginning of the prophecy of Isaiah 53, which spoke of the One who would be despised, rejected, and hated by men. This Christ who had displayed so much care for the hearts of fallen and hurting people was only beginning to feel the rebellion and hatred of His own creation. And Peter watched.

A GROWING PRESSURE

Years ago, George Barna released a book on the changing dynamics of the evangelical church in America. He described survey results that showed a weakening commitment to Scripture and a growing departure from the historic commitment of church members to the institutional local church. His studies revealed a trend that had been steadily growing over time—a development that had occurred almost imperceptibly. As valuable as the information was, what intrigued me most was the book's title, a title that so graphically described the condition of the church: *The Frog in the Kettle*.

The title was rooted in the real-world principle that if you put a frog in a pan of steaming hot water, the frog will instantly jump out to safety. If you take the same frog, however, and put it in tepid water, then slowly increase the heat in gradual increments, the frog will adjust with the heat of the water—all the way to its death. The frog will boil to death without realizing the ever-growing danger. That, Barna contended, was the dangerous condition in which the church found itself—slowly, almost imperceptibly, adapting to its surroundings until it no longer contained the life it had been granted in Christ.

Peter is just like a frog in a kettle. The heat keeps increasing, and he doesn't have the sense or wisdom or discernment to jump to safety. And as the pressure grows, he keeps trying to adjust until it is too late—and he is crushed under the pressure of his own failure and lack of wisdom. The pressure begins innocently enough—a young girl confronts him first! But Peter will try to adapt and adjust until the heat overwhelms him, and he fails the most significant test of his life.

Test #1—A Servant Girl

As Peter was below in the courtyard, one of the servant-girls of the high priest came, and seeing Peter warming himself, she looked at him and said, "You also were with Jesus the Nazarene." But he denied it, saying, "I neither know nor understand what you are talking about." And he went out onto the porch (Mark 14:66–68).

In the sad and confused heart of Simon Peter, we see a powerful contradiction. He was ready to go to battle with swords when the Roman troops and temple guards showed up in the garden, but he wasn't ready for a guerilla raid cleverly disguised in the form of this young woman. He wasn't ready for a battle of wits with a servant girl.

When she steps up and accuses Peter of having been a close associate of the Nazarene, the faltering disciple denies Christ by feigning ignorance. "What? Me? I don't understand what you are talking about!" Peter is in deep trouble—and continues to make all the wrong choices as the water temperature in his personal kettle is being turned up.

Test #2—Another Maid

The servant-girl saw him, and began once more to say to the bystanders, "This is one of them!" (Mark 14:69).
A little later, another saw him and said, "You are one of them too!" But Peter said, "Man, I am not!" (Luke 22:58).

"A little later" means that about an hour had passed—but Simon is still there! This time, another servant joins this maid in raising the accusation once more, and this time Peter strengthens his denial even further by claiming that he had never even been associated with Jesus. As the number of accusations increases, so does the temperature of the water in the kettle.

Test #3—The Rest

But again he denied it. And after a little while the bystanders were again saying to Peter, "Surely you are one of them, for you are a Galilean too." But he began to curse and swear, "I do not know this man you are talking about!" (Mark 14:70–71).

Fascinating, isn't it, that John 18:26 reveals that one of the members of the crowd at the fire is a relative of Malchus—the man Peter had attacked in the garden! They identify his Galilean dialect and accuse him of being a friend of Christ, so Simon alters his speech to pursue further self-protection. In Mark 14:71, we read that he even resorted to curses and swearing! He now has denied everything—knowledge of Christ, relationship with Christ, and the impact of Christ in his life.

The downward spiral is now complete. He has moved from self-confidence to carelessness and from carelessness to self-assertion. Now Peter builds on that self-assertion by collapsing into fear and, ultimately, denial. What he had promised in self-confidence he would not be able to pull off. It is the failure that comes when we think that in some way we can serve God in our own strength. Jesus meant it when He said, "Without Me you can do nothing (John 15:5)." Peter would now have to take the heat for his decisions and failures.

A REALIZED FAILURE

We call them "aha moments"—those instantaneous flashpoints of clarity that bring the moment into perspective. The proverbial light bulb goes on over our heads, and in that "aha moment," we receive understanding of something that had been muddy and unclear before. Such a moment had come years earlier when Peter, tired and grumpy from a long night of fishing the Galilee, was instructed by a Nazarene carpenter to launch into the deep portion of the lake for a catch. As he reluctantly lowered his net, Simon felt as if he were on a fool's errand—until the net began to burst from the fish it contained, and he had to call his partners (James and John) to come and help with the magnificent catch. This tangible evidence of the impossible, coupled with the testimony of Simon's brother (Andrew), brought new insight to the heart of the rough-hewn fisherman. He realized the identity of the traveling Rabbi and declared, "Go away from me Lord, for I am a sinful man!" (Luke 5:8). Aha moment indeed! Two insights planted themselves in the very front of His mind—Jesus was Messiah, and Simon was sinful.

Since that life-changing moment some three years earlier, Peter had seen plenty of evidence to continually confirm both of those realities. But now things have turned in a dramatically ugly way. Peter has cut himself adrift from the Captain of his heart and is about to experience two more realities that will arrest his attention and consume his thinking for the next days—which would be the darkest of his life.

The Cock Crows

But Peter said, "Man, I do not know what you are talking about." Immediately, while he was still speaking, a rooster crowed (Luke 22:60).

Immediately a rooster crowed a second time. And Peter remembered how Jesus had made the remark to him, "Before a rooster crows twice, you will deny Me three times." And he began to weep (Mark 14:72).

Now the penny drops. The moment is cold and dark, but Peter's mind is alive with realization. The rooster's crow has brought him crashing back to his senses, and the ignored warnings now replay themselves in his mind on a continuous loop. Jesus had warned, Peter had ignored. Jesus had challenged, Peter had ignored. Jesus had protected, Peter had ignored. And as Jesus was on trial, Peter once again had ignored the fact of his own weakness and now has fallen. Not once. Not twice. Three times. Exactly as Jesus had warned and challenged and sought to protect.

This instant realization produces a flood of emotions in Peter. His fear has now been overtaken by regret. His self-reliance has been consumed by guilt. His lack of preparation has resulted in deep personal failure, and his emotions run like whitewater— emerging from his broken heart as tears of weeping and grief. All his promises—failed. All his self-confidence—broken. All his values and beliefs—violated. In a moment, he feels his treason and turns away to sob in his suffering. And when he does, he sees the Master—and the Master sees him.

The Christ Looks

The Lord turned and looked at Peter. And Peter remembered the word of the Lord, how He had told him, "Before a rooster crows today, you will deny Me three times." And he went out and wept bitterly (Luke 22:61–62).

Much has been made of this very intimate moment of anguish. Some say that Jesus looked at Peter in disappointment, as if to say, "Tsk, tsk. Here he goes again." I understand that look. As a boy, I dreaded more than anything else the thought that I might disappoint my father. Others speculate that the look of Christ was one of judgment. So was it a look of scorn to intensify Peter's guilt, or a look of pity at the pathetic man and his pathetically broken heart?

Luke doesn't describe Jesus' look or qualify its tone or temper. Yet Luke has repeatedly described in his gospel record the heart behind that look. The heart of the Shepherd that leaves the ninety-nine and goes seeking for the one lost sheep—a wandering sheep like Peter. The heart of the Father, standing at the road looking lovingly into the horizon for the familiar figure of His very own prodigal son—a wayward son like Peter. It is this evidence that compels my heart to believe that the look of Jesus was one of profound sadness and deep concern. Jesus knew all that Peter would endure that dark night and longed to reach to him. I believe the look was one of grace and not disgust. A gaze of mercy to a hear desperately needing it—for all Peter sees is the guilt of his reckl choices and their consequences. All he sees is his own failure. dark night of his soul has begun. He has denied his Lord.

Peter was not alone in his failure. It feels all too familiar to us as we fail our Christ and our relationships by making an accommodation that is committed to nothing more than just getting by. In the epic miniseries *Lonesome Dove*, former Texas Ranger Jake Spoon hooks up with a small band to try to safely make it through the Oklahoma Territory. He comfortably fits in, adjusting to this cutthroat element that he would have at one time arrested and hung. Finally, after the murders and rustlings and savagery of these men have taken a number of lives, Spoon's former Ranger partners, Woodrow Call and Augustus McCrae, catch the marauding group of killers. As they prepare to hang their friend, Spoon pleads by saying he wasn't part of it all, that his intention was to split from them. That he was just trying to get through.

Gus tells him, "Sorry Jake. But you crossed the line."

Jake's response? "I didn't see no line, Gus." That is what a growing pressure does. It blinds us to our choices and their implications, making us people of the moment who don't stop to consider the long-term consequences of our choices. We become vacuous hearts—"just trying to get through."

Thankfully, Jesus does not hang us for our failures. He offers us forgiveness and grace—the same forgiveness and grace He would offer to Peter as the Master restored His fallen disciple to service. The three denials of Peter in John 19 were answered by three declarations of love for Christ on the shores of the Galilee in John 21—and Peter moved forward, forgiven. He was restored to his position of leadership and became the instrument of the Savior in preaching the great Pentecost sermon that gave birth to the church—the body of Christ. Though second chances are not always to be assumed, Peter graciously received one. As did I.

Some months ago, I found that I was thinking regularly about my friend Tom and all that we had shared together as boys growing up in the hills of West Virginia. Finally, I got online and started searching until I found my boyhood friend's current address and phone number. With great hesitation I called, not knowing what the response would be. When Tom answered the phone, I didn't even recognize his voice—nor did he recognize mine. But when I told him who I was, an amazing thing happened. It was as if we picked back up where we had left off thirty years ago. I so deeply regret the loss of a friend for so many years but am so grateful for a friend who forgives. That is the kind of friend Jesus was to Peter as well—and is to us. A friend who forgives, who lays down His life for His friends, and who sticks closer than a brother. A friend we often deny but never stop needing in our lives. The hymn writer captured it well:

What a friend we have in Jesus,
All our sins and griefs to bear!
What a privilege to carry
Everything to God in prayer!
O, what peace we often forfeit,
O what needless pain we bear,
All because we do not carry
Everything to God in prayer.

Loving Christ, I long to see Your look of grace and mercy
but fear the failures of my soul that might produce it.
Forgive me for all my bluster and self-sufficiency. Teach

my heart the value of communion with You in secret that prepares me for the challenges and temptations that produce all-too-public failures. Teach me to listen to You, to lean upon You, to love You, and to learn from You—that I might stand for You in Your strength. Teach me to repent when I fail and to rejoice when I learn to stand in You. Loving Christ, I long to see Your look of grace and mercy and hear You say, "Well done."

SIX

TRIED BY HIS ENEMIES

Perry Mason was the man. He was brilliant, articulate, composed, and able to pull a legal rabbit out of his hat whenever all seemed lost. It was fascinating to watch as justice always prevailed in the television courtrooms where Mason defended innocent clients who had been wrongly charged. You almost had to feel a little sorry for his weekly opponent, prosecutor Hamilton Burger (yes, that's right—Perry Mason turned him into "hamburger"). He could never win. His case could be a dead mortal lock, and Mason would win anyway. It had nothing to do with Burger's lawyering skills and everything to do with justice and right prevailing. The guilty were always uncovered and the falsely accused always went free in an ongoing statement of what American justice should be like.

In dramatic contrast to that, however, was a film that came out in 2003 entitled *Runaway Jury,* starring Gene Hackman, Dustin Hoffman, and John Cusack. It was the tale of modern "justice," as a high-profile case went to court with a wrongful death civil lawsuit against a gun manufacturer. To make a favorable verdict a certainty, the gun manufacturer hired Hackman's character, a high-octane jury consultant. His job, along with his team of detectives, techies, and psychologists, was to analyze the jury for weak points—places in their lives, families, or backgrounds that could be manipulated. Ways that their jury votes could be bought, pressured, or turned in the favor of the gun company (in this case, the accused). For much of the film, a battle for justice ensues due to the fact that to Hackman's great surprise, there is another force in play that is also trying to move the jury in a direction that would favor the plaintiff—a woman whose husband has been murdered by a man using a gun made by the defending gun company. It is a taut, finely tuned John Grisham courtroom thriller—and I found it disturbing. The writing and acting were both great, and the story was interesting. What bothered me was the realization of how vulnerable the justice system seemed to be to manipulation.

In fact, I found myself wondering if real justice was even possible anymore. The days of Perry Mason and black-and-white justice seem a distant memory that cannot be recaptured. It made me long for simpler times when issues were more clear-cut and justice (along with its companion, liberty), as described in the Pledge of Allegiance, was available to all.

Justice, however, is not merely a victim of clever and diabolical minds in the modern and postmodern world. It is not the victim of cutting-edge technology or ruthless legal eagles. Justice is ultimately a hard needle to thread, because we live in a world that is inherently unjust—a fact that was proven in a thoroughly rigged trial two thousand years ago when the Righteous Judge of the earth was tried in a kangaroo court and found guilty on trumped-up charges through the testimony of false witnesses. Tragically, injustice in courtrooms is nothing new, and we will see that as the Christ is tried by His enemies.

THE RELIGIOUS TRIAL

So the Roman cohort and the commander and the officers of
the Jews, arrested Jesus and bound Him, and led Him to Annas

first; for he was father-in-law of Caiaphas, who was high priest that year. Now Caiaphas was the one who had advised the Jews that it was expedient for one man to die on behalf of the people (John 18:12–14).

The Bible doesn't record for us the events that occurred as the party moved from Gethsemane to the site of the first trial, but we can imagine that it was not a gentle stroll in which Christ was treated with kindness and consideration. Ironically, the soldiers choose to bind Jesus, though they have Him seriously outnumbered. Perhaps they had heard the stories of Jesus' miraculous powers, and they thought that by binding His hands His power could be controlled. Obviously they had no real idea who they were dealing with—many of our Lord's miracles had been performed at the command of His word without any use of His hands! Finally they arrive at the home of Annas, and the night of unjust, illegal trials begins.

Step One: Before Annas

The high priest then questioned Jesus about His disciples, and about His teaching. Jesus answered him, "I have spoken openly to the world; I always taught in synagogues and in the temple, where all the Jews come together; and I spoke nothing in secret. Why do you question Me? Question those who have heard what I spoke to them; they know what I said." When He had said this, one of the officers standing nearby struck Jesus, saying, "Is that the way You answer the high priest?" Jesus answered him, "If I have spoken wrongly, testify of the wrong; but if rightly, why do you strike Me?" (John 18:19–23).

Annas was the real power behind the religious establishment in the days of Christ. For years he had held the authority of the office of high priest, either personally, through his sons, or through his sons-in-law. At this time, he ruled through the puppet leadership of his son-in-law Caiaphas. Additionally, Annas controlled the temple concessions and the corruption those concessions had produced. Use of temple coin instead of the coin of the realm had forced the people to trade money at drastically unfair exchange rates. They were then forced to purchase sacrificial animals at ridiculously inflated prices. These elements combined to produce lavish wealth for Annas and his cronies—and must have caused Annas to hate Jesus and long for revenge against Him.

Just days before, Christ had torn through the temple concession area with a whip—overturning tables of coins and releasing potential sales items (sacrificial birds and animals). Worse, He had declared Annas and his crowd corrupt and apostate for producing such a disgraceful situation as the concessions at the temple. Now Jesus has been delivered into his hands, and Annas is thrilled with the opportunity to exact revenge on his personal tormentor. Though one of the keepers of the laws of Israel, Annas completely ignores the legal requirements for a just trial, violating at least four of the guidelines established for proper legal actions:

1. No prisoner could be called on to testify against himself. "The high priest then questioned Jesus about His disciples, and about His teaching" (John 18:19).
2. No prisoner could be struck while in custody awaiting trial or during the trial itself. "When He had said this, one of the officers standing nearby struck Jesus" (John 18:22).
3. No trial could be held at night—yet it is deep in the night as they arrive at Annas's home.

4. At least two days had to expire between the trial and the execution of sentence—but in only a few hours the innocent Christ will be hanging on a cross.

From the very outset of the proceedings, the eternally just Judge of all the earth is treated with treachery and injustice—by those whose responsibility it was to ensure that justice prevailed! Annas has seen and heard all he cares about. In his mind, the innocence or guilt of the Christ is not an issue—creating justifiable cause for execution is his only concern. Convinced that he has all he needs, Annas dispatches Jesus to Caiaphas in order for the "real" trials to begin.

Step Two: Before Caiaphas

So Annas sent Him bound to Caiaphas the high priest (John 18:24).

Trying to get inside the head of Caiaphas is not the easiest task in the world. When I was in college, our drama department presented a play about the passion events, and I was cast in the role of Caiaphas, the high priest. It was challenging in many ways, but perhaps the greatest challenge was trying to be fair in representing the actions and motives of this much-reviled religious leader. I came out of the experience feeling precious little pity for Caiaphas and much dislike for this political wolf in the sheep's clothing of a religious leader.

John does not give us a record of the interrogation before Caiaphas, but that is at least in part because his vote was secondary to the vote of Annas. But what is most significant here is the satisfaction that Caiaphas must have felt. Notice that in John 18:14 we read, "Now Caiaphas was the one who had advised the Jews that it was expedient for one man to die on behalf of the people." He was involved in the private plan to manipulate the public away from its fascination with Jesus and toward a more hostile perspective. The actual comments are found in John 11:49–50: "But one of them, Caiaphas, who was high priest that year, said to them, 'You know nothing at all, nor do you take into account that it is expedient for you that one man die for the people, and that the whole nation not perish.'"

On the face of it, it might appear that Caiaphas was concerned for the welfare of the people. After all, Rome had the reputation of an "iron heel" for a reason. Rebellion was regularly smashed into submission by the force of the Roman legions. If the people were to continue to grow in their clamoring for the Nazarene prophet to be their king, only bad would come from it. Thousands had died in Israel already because of Roman authority that was determined to keep control of the volatile region. Certainly there was cause for concern.

In reality, however, Caiaphas, much like the despised Herods, was a political power broker who was more concerned with protecting his substantial position than he was with protecting the people. He had no real interest in determining the legitimacy of Christ's claims; he was simply trying to solve a problem and remove a growing annoyance. The coming trials are only to provide the pretense of legitimacy. In the mind of Caiaphas, the verdict is predetermined. What is so astounding is that this decision has been made in the face of three years of evidence that calls for a response, and that evidence has grown significantly by the recent events surrounding the raising of Lazarus from the dead. Caiaphas was not a victim, a pawn, or a puppet—he was acting on the basis of a willful rejection of the evidence and the Christ that evidence proclaimed.

Caiaphas, well satisfied in having accomplished his goals, calls for a meeting of the Sanhedrin to declare the verdict that has already been decided.

Step Three: Before the Sanhedrin

The Sanhedrin was an ecclesiastical body representing the various factions of religious thinking in that day as well as leading laymen of the community. The people looked to them to administer justice and fairness and to dispense wisdom that would be consistent with Old Testament law. Their practices this night would deny that trust and show them to be men of questionable character and motive. The entire pattern of their processes exposes a commitment to corruption.

- They seek false witnesses in order to condemn the One who is the physical embodiment of truth: "Now the chief priests and the whole Council kept trying to obtain false testimony against Jesus, so that they might put Him to death. They did not find any, even though many false witnesses came forward. But later on two came forward, and said, 'This man stated, "I am able to destroy the temple of God and to rebuild it in three days"'" (Matthew 26:59–61).

- Once again, they seek to force Jesus into testifying against Himself, this time by taking God's name in an oath: "The high priest stood up and said to Him, 'Do You not answer? What is it that these men are testifying against You?' But Jesus kept silent. And the high priest said to Him, 'I adjure You by the living God, that You tell us whether You are the Christ, the Son of God'" (Matthew 26:62–63).

- Jesus makes His claim of divine Sonship: "Jesus said to him, 'You have said it yourself; nevertheless I tell you, hereafter you will see THE SON OF MAN SITTING AT THE RIGHT HAND OF POWER, and COMING ON THE CLOUDS OF HEAVEN'" (Matthew 26:64).

- Jesus is accused of blasphemy, but there is no attempt made to either prove or disprove the charges—only to condemn His claims. The death penalty is declared by the assembled council, though there has been no legal case built for the charges: "Then the high priest tore his robes and said, 'He has blasphemed! What further need do we have of witnesses? Behold, you have now heard the blasphemy; what do you think?'" They answered, 'He deserves death!'" (Matthew 26:65–66).

- More illegal beatings and mockery occur—all under the watchful and approving eye of Caiaphas the high priest and the Sanhedrin—the so-called guardians of justice: "Then they spat in His face and beat Him with their fists; and others slapped Him, and said, 'Prophesy to us, You Christ; who is the one who hit You?'" (Matthew 26:67–68).

With that, the religious trials have ended. The fly in the buttermilk for the Sanhedrin, however, is that as an occupied country under Roman rule they can call for the death penalty, but they cannot carry it out. Only Rome has that authority. This requires them now to seek that approval from the civil authority: Pontius Pilate, the Roman procurator (or governor) of Judea. In the end, they seek to legitimize their illegal actions by waiting until morning to finalize their verdict and then send Jesus away for civil trial before Pilate.

THE CIVIL TRIAL

Now when morning came, all the chief priests and the elders of the people conferred together against Jesus to put Him to death; and they bound Him, and led Him away and delivered Him to Pilate the governor (Matthew 27:1–2).

With the beginning of the civil trials, an entirely new set of conditions and qualifiers comes into play—along with a new set of participants. Matthew 27:2 tells us that the leaders of the Sanhedrin led Jesus to stand civil trial before Pilate, but at that point, Luke's gospel record interjects a scene that is just plain pathetic. Of the four gospels, only Luke reveals that Jesus was initially brought to Pilate, and he refused to hear the case. The grounds? Because Jesus was from Galilee, He would fall under the jurisdiction of Herod (Luke 23:6), who was responsible for that region of Palestine. This gave him an accessible escape hatch for a problem he didn't want to have to deal with and put a thorn in the side of a significant political enemy. This allows us to see the reality that Pilate is already ducking this powder-keg issue, showing us very early in the proceedings his general weakness of character. More significantly, however, it insures that both the Jewish and Roman legal systems will participate in this travesty, so that Jew and Gentile alike are accountable for their rejection of the Christ.

Step Four: Before Herod

In this hastily called audience between the ceremonial king of the Jews and the actual King of kings, what are most significant are the things that *don't* happen:

- Herod doesn't get to see a miracle: "Now Herod was very glad when he saw Jesus; for he had wanted to see Him for a long time because he had been hearing about Him, and was hoping to see some sign performed by Him" (Luke 23:8).

- Herod doesn't receive answers to his questions: "And he questioned Him at some length; but He answered him nothing" (Luke 23:9).

- Herod doesn't attempt to uncover the real truth: "And the chief priests and the scribes were standing there, accusing Him vehemently" (Luke 23:10).

- Herod makes no attempt to bring an end to this injustice but instead allows the grotesque and shameful treatment of Christ to continue with renewed enthusiasm: "And Herod with his soldiers, after treating Him with contempt and mocking Him, dressed Him in a gorgeous robe and sent Him back to Pilate" (Luke 23:11).

Having received no satisfaction from the exercise, Herod, with great frustration and disappointment, sends Jesus back to Pilate. The fascinating reality of this is that each of the men who have examined Christ to this point have allowed his own personal goals and agenda to dictate his reaction to the Son of God.

- Annas responded on the basis of self-interest, desiring to protect the temple concessions he controlled.
- Caiaphas responded on the basis of self-preservation, desiring to protect his fragile position of leadership.
- Herod responded on the basis of self-seeking, only desiring a moment or two of entertainment.

As Herod dispatches Jesus back to Pilate for trial, an interesting phenomenon occurs. These two men on opposite sides of the political aisle find themselves now connected, in fact and in history. Luke says, "Now Herod and Pilate became friends with one another that very day; for before they had been enemies with each other" (Luke 23:12). A friendship forged out of injustice, convenience, and expediency. With friends like this, who needs enemies?

Step Five: Before Pilate

On an episode of the television series *The West Wing*, President Josiah Bartlet, in a discussion with a psychologist, is defending his choices as the leader of the free world and says, "I think I've made tough choices." The psychologist responds, "I think Abraham Lincoln did what he thought was right, knowing it might cost him half the nation. And you don't do what you think is right because it might cost you Michigan's electoral votes."

Choices under pressure reveal character. If leadership is to accomplish anything, it must display true depth of character—and never is that character more necessary than in times of crisis.

Pontius Pilate, procurator of Judea, is about to enter a time of crisis that will reveal his character for the vacuum that it is—a poverty of integrity that will ultimately show that he fears people more than God. Now, to be fair, this is not his first crisis. In his time of rule in Judea, he has already had to enact the art of brinkmanship during three public crises:

- He brought the Roman standards into the shadow of the temple in Jerusalem—standards that bore the graven image of Caesar as god. The people rioted for five days until Pilate caved in and removed the standards.

- He used *korban* money—dedicated for the use of the temple—to build an aqueduct. The resulting riots were put down with merciless beatings.
- He brought into the city votive shields, once again bearing Caesar's image.

The bloody outcomes of these riots had not played well in Rome, and Pilate knew that another mishandled crisis could well be his last. So of course this was the last thing he wanted to happen—Jesus was brought back to him with the religious leaders demanding the death penalty for crimes Pilate didn't even understand! Now, under pressure, Pilate will cave in tragically. Through the course of the trial, several key themes continue to percolate to the surface:

- Pilate will try to dodge the issue
- the pressure of the religious leaders will be relentless
- the majesty of Christ will be displayed
- God's plan will be accomplished

In it all, the regal Christ will continue to suffer mercilessly at the hands of the hate-filled priests, the angry mob, and the cowardly Pilate—and the contrast could not be more stunning. As Morris said, "As you contrast Christ's humble majesty from Pilate's proud majesty, all other actions recede from attention." The topic of discussion assures this focus, for the subject is kingship. Ultimately this is not a confrontation between Christ and Pilate but rather between Christ and Caesar. The threat is not mere or imagined—it is legitimate. Christ is King, and the fact that He is about to be executed does not diminish His glory. Nor does the fact that Pilate will clearly discern Christ's innocence diminish the cowardice he displays by condemning the Savior in the face of that innocence. As the trial unfolds in John 18, it proceeds with a series of questions and their resultant answers—and unveils significant principles that we must consider as well.

Question #1—"Are You the King of the Jews?" (v. 33). This first question is in all four gospel records and is stunning when you consider what Pilate is looking at. Jesus has already endured countless beatings and is showing the effects of a night of savagery inflicted upon Him. With this question, Jesus reverses the roles and becomes the interrogator: "Are you saying this on your own initiative, or did others tell you about Me?" (v. 34). If Pilate were seeking a political solution to the problem, he would be disappointed, but that is not the point. The point in Jesus' rebuttal is to challenge Pilate to decision. In effect He says, "Pilate, you must make up your own mind. What's your response?" Though Pilate tries to duck the issue by shifting responsibility for the trial to the Jewish leaders, he cannot. He must decide. Pilate must choose.

Question #2—"What have You done?" (v. 35b). Jesus responds with a clear description of the kingdom that the Sanhedrin has so badly misrepresented. "Jesus answered, 'My kingdom is not of this world. If My kingdom were of this world, then My servants would be fighting so that I would not be handed over to the Jews; but as it is, My kingdom is not of this realm'" (v. 36). They had rejected the rule of Christ in their hearts, but it was not too late for Pilate—not yet. The principle? What kingdom will own your allegiance? You cannot have a divided heart—either Christ will be your king or not. Which will it be?

Question #3—"So You are a king?" (v. 37a). Jesus' answer pulls Pilate ever closer to decision. Christ affirms, "You say *correctly* that I am a king. For this I have been born, and for this I have come into the world, to testify to the truth. Everyone who is of the truth hears My voice" (v. 37b, emphasis added). Christ entered the world with purpose, and that purpose would find its destiny on Pilate's portico. Christ had come into the world with divine interest and a divine mission. The principle? Pilate needs to look beyond kings and kingdoms and see the true and living God! The God of truth beckoned him. What would Pilate do?

Question #4—"What is truth?" (v. 38). In response to Jesus' call to embrace truth, Pilate sarcastically questions whether such a thing as truth even exists! The principle is that truth is the ultimate test of our lives, and it can only be found in the God of truth. Perhaps that is why there is such an absence of justice in our culture today—we dismissed justice from the cultural landscape when we determined to be a "truth-optional" society. The difference between *Runaway Jury* and Perry Mason is found therein. It is the difference between subjective, situational morality and the belief in an absolute truth. Pilate had a choice—and under pressure he chose poorly. He announced to the waiting crowd the obvious and clear innocence of Jesus Christ but refused to take action on that. It was an assertion that was not a conviction. It was a decision without heart or passion—and it would quickly go away.

HUMANITY'S GREATEST INJUSTICE

Step Six: Before History

During the Cuban Missile Crisis of 1962, on the floor of the United Nations, Adlai Stevenson pressured the ambassador of the Soviet Union to answer questions about the presence of nuclear missiles in Cuba. The ambassador responded by saying he was not in an American courtroom and would not be questioned as if he were. Stevenson responded, "Sir, you are in the court of public opinion." The world was watching breathlessly, waiting for the drama to play itself out.

Pilate did not just stand in the court of Roman authority or in the court of the Praetorium in his home in Jerusalem or even in the court of the Sanhedrin and its agenda. He likewise was not in the court of public opinion. It was the court of history, and in the end, it was not Jesus Christ but Pontius Pilate himself who was on trial. Trying to escape, he attempted to satiate the crowd. He offered to execute a notorious criminal, Barabbas, and set Christ free (John 18:39–40). When the crowd refused the bone he tried to throw their way, Pilate had Christ savagely beaten, hoping to elicit some pity for this broken and battered "victim" of public opinion turned ugly (John 19:1–4). Displaying what was left of the brutalized Christ, complete with the mockery of a purple robe and crown of thorns, he could only say, *"Ecce homo"* ("Behold, the Man") (v. 5).

In the end, however, the crowd, like sharks, had sensed blood in the water and demanded death for the Prince of life. Pilate, despite urgings from his troubled wife and the conclusions of his own conscience, condemned Christ to death—and truth and justice with Him. In John 19:15–16, the sad tale finds its conclusion:

> *So they cried out, "Away with Him, away with Him, crucify Him!" Pilate said to them, "Shall I crucify your King?" The chief priests answered, "We have no king but Caesar." So he then handed Him over to them to be crucified (John 19:15–16).*

The Jewish leaders and the Roman leader who lacked leadership ability conspired to condemn the Son of God to death by crucifixion. It was humanity's greatest injustice, Pilate's darkest moment, the Sanhedrin's most severe shame, and God's perfect purpose in the most amazing of all expressions of God's rescue mission for a lost race. By human evil, the holiness of God was being accomplished. By human hate, God's most complete declaration of love took form. The hymn writer pens:

> *"Man of Sorrows!" what a name*
> *For the Son of God, Who came*
> *Ruined sinners to reclaim.*
> *Hallelujah! What a Savior!*

Living Lord, the Judge of the earth and the God of truth, thank You for accepting injustice so that I could escape the justice and judgment that I deserved. Thank You for allowing lies to be told about You so that You could forgive the truth about me. Thank You for embracing the mistreatment of humanity so that You might pour out Your grace upon me. Upon us. Thank You for becoming the Man of Sorrows so that I might be able to experience joys forevermore. Thank You. Amen.

SEVEN

SURROUNDED BY THE CROWD

On my first trip to Israel, my eyes were wide most of the time and my mouth hung open in amazement at all that I saw and experienced. Walking in the land of the Bible, seeing the places where the events of Scripture took place, understanding more clearly the three-dimensional environment in which history's most significant happenings occurred was, well, hard to process. I spent an awful lot of the time feeling like I needed more RAM in my head, because what I was seeing felt like trying to take a drink from a fire hydrant. Thrill upon thrill followed each new day as the Bible came alive in a fresh new way. From Caesarea by the Sea to Mount Carmel to Megiddo to Capernaum to Jerusalem to Ein Gedi to Masada—it was truly the trip of a lifetime. Except for one particular day.

The day we walked the Via Dolorosa (the actual route Christ followed to the cross) was surprisingly disappointing. First, our guide informed us that Christ's real path to the cross was about twenty-five feet underground—buried beneath two thousand years of history piling onto the Old City of Jerusalem. Then came the walk itself, which seemed—well—too tame. People were polite. Occasional groups of pilgrims would pass by carrying signs or crosses. Other groups softly sang hymns or offered prayers at the various Stations of the Cross. Those different liturgical stages of the cross felt almost sterile and ceremonial. It was quiet, hushed, almost worshipful, and it all felt completely . . . wrong.

When Jesus trod the Via Dolorosa (the Way of Suffering), it was anything but sterile or polite. It was far from ceremonial. We need to see *that* Via Dolorosa—the dangerous, violent, hate-filled one. To do that, we must step into the crowd that lined the way on that sun-drenched morning in Jerusalem two thousand years ago. Imagine it as it was—a narrow, stone-covered street that was actually little more than an alley. The pathway was barely wide enough to accommodate the condemned men, their crosses, and the soldiers that accompanied them, let alone the mobs that had gathered to see (and be entertained by) this spectacle. As Jesus walks that lonely road to the cross, we must see and hear what the crowd that day saw and heard. And through the course of this death march, several things will grasp our hearts and demand our attention—things we cannot merely observe and then turn our gaze away from. Things we must think through. Things we must respond to.

> *So he [Pilate] then handed Him over to them to be crucified. They took Jesus, therefore, and He went out, bearing His own cross, to the place called the Place of a Skull, which is called in Hebrew, Golgotha (John 19:16–17).*

First, let's be reminded of the scene before us, because it is vital that we keep that scene in focus. What has led to this moment?

- It has been about two and a half hours since Jesus was first brought to stand trial before Pilate, and it has been about fourteen and a half hours since the Last Supper began in the upper room. Now, in the harsh light of the Judean morning, those events must have seemed an eternity ago. The relative peace and calm of the previous evening have been replaced by an unspeakable hostility as people relish the suffering of an innocent man.

- Jesus has endured five illegal trials and at least four savage and merciless beatings. Physically, Christ is in terrible condition, fulfilling the awful prophecy of Isaiah that His appearance would be so marred that people would turn their head rather than look at Him (Isaiah 53:3). The clubs, fists, thorns, and cat-of-nine-tails have done their work—and Christ has been battered beyond human recognition. Emotionally, Jesus has suffered betrayal by one disciple, been denied by another, and abandoned by all. Spiritually, the agony of the Gethsemane experience has increased His sufferings exponentially. The Son of God is certainly in the midst of bearing our griefs and carrying our sorrows (Isaiah 53:4).

Now the trials have come to a close, and it is time to walk the long, painful road to Golgotha. Upon the decision to execute Christ, Pilate would have declared, *"Illum duci ad crucem placet."* ("This man should be taken to a cross.") He would have then turned to the centurion in charge of the execution team and said, *"I, miles, expedi crucem."* ("Go, soldier, and prepare the cross.") As the cross is prepared, history and tradition combine to provide evidence that there were basically three types of crosses used for executions carried out by Rome:

- the St. Andrew's cross (an X-shaped cross)
- the Crux Commissa (a T-shaped cross)
- the Latin cross that has become the traditional type used as a symbol of Christianity

The most common of these (and what no doubt was used) was the Latin (traditional) cross, which was made up of two pieces—a standard (the upright piece) and a patibulum (the crosspiece). If, in fact, Jesus' cross was the Latin cross, it is likely that He carried only the patibulum. He would have been tied to it in order to bear it upon His shoulders for the long walk to the Place of the Skull. The weight of the crosspiece alone would have been considerable, and the rough-hewn wood must have been painful upon Christ's back, ripped and torn by the whippings He had received through the course of the trials.

By now, it is about 8:30 a.m. The streets are already filled with people crowding into the city to make last-minute preparations for the Passover feast that would begin that evening at sunset. The word is just starting to spread that an execution is underway. As Jesus is led away, the entourage would have contained the three condemned men carrying their crosses, a quaternion (a group of four) of soldiers for each condemned man, and about 120 soldiers to provide crowd control as the group moved its way through the gathering mobs.

In it all, Jesus suffers. The crown of thorns, the cross and what it means, the crowds and their mockery—all add to the horror of the moment. Yet His suffering is made all the more amazing by the ultimate truth that this is a voluntary sacrifice. Jesus said, "For this reason the Father loves Me, because I lay down My life so that I may take it again. No one has taken it away from Me, but I lay it down on My own initiative" (John 10:17–18). It is a bleeding portrait of the strength of deity, the power of divine love, and the majesty of grace. It is the Lamb of God taking away the sins of the world.

As the grim entourage moved its way slowly through the early morning streets of Jerusalem, the responses of the crowd must have been very diverse. Some mocked, some were shocked, some wept, some were confused—but all watched. We watch with them, and first we see one man who began that day simply as another watcher in the crowd, a casual observer, who ended the day as an unwilling participant.

A MAN

When they led Him away, they seized a man, Simon of Cyrene, coming in from the country, and placed on him the cross to carry behind Jesus (Luke 23:26).

As was common for a condemned man, Jesus carried His cross—but not for long. The physical suffering of the last fifteen hours or so has taken its toll. The garden agony, the beatings, the sleepless night on trial, being dragged all over town, even the weight of the wood itself—all contribute to the weakness and fatigue He now feels. Apparently decimated by all these things, Christ stumbles (perhaps several times) under the burden of the cross. As a result, the soldiers in charge of Jesus' execution draft someone to carry the cross for Him.

This was Roman law, sometimes called "the tap of the spear." A Roman soldier could compel anyone to carry a load for him for the space of a mile simply by tapping his victim on the shoulder with his spear. This practice was despised by occupied countries, for it reinforced their humiliation and disgrace as a conquered people—a reality that makes it all the more remarkable that Jesus chose that very practice as an opportunity to teach grace, compassion, and a servant's heart to His followers. Jesus' words? "Whoever forces you to go one mile, go with him two" (Matthew 5:41). Take a servant's heart without shame or anger, but display love in acts of service. That principle was foreign to the thinking of the subjugated people of Israel. Yet, once again, Jesus' teaching that at first blush sounded counterintuitive was, in fact, the very life He was modeling—the model of One who did not come to be served, but to serve and to give His life a ransom for many.

Now, out of the throngs crowding into this little passageway, one person is going to be selected as one of the soldiers in Jesus' quaternion reaches into the mass of watching people and conscripts one man with the tap of the spear: Simon of Cyrene.

His Name

It would appear that Simon was a Jew from Cyrene, a town in Libya near the Mediterranean Sea and the city of Tripoli. Undoubtedly, Simon had come to Jerusalem as a Jewish pilgrim desiring to celebrate the feast of Passover. He probably knew nothing of what had been happening in the past months and days as Jesus had become increasingly controversial and, therefore, increasingly a threat to the religious establishment of Israel. As a basic innocent bystander, Simon was forced to get involved in the ugly scene that he had stumbled onto while entering the city. Having apparently come to Jerusalem to privately worship as a participant at the feast, Simon finds himself in the swirling cauldron of some very public events. Having come to offer the paschal lamb, he unknowingly will aid in the sacrifice of God's true Passover.

His Situation

Simon was forced against his will to carry the cross of Jesus, providing a dramatic contrast between his deed and the choices of a true disciple of Christ:

Simon	*Disciple*
Served by force	Serves by choice

Served to speed death	Serves to aid life
Served as an inconvenience	Serves as a lifestyle
Served in embarrassment	Serves with joy

This is the focus of Christ's words in Matthew 16, as He describes the heart and commitment of a true disciple—a commitment that Simon has, at this point, not embraced.

Then Jesus said to His disciples, "If anyone wishes to come after Me, he must deny himself, and take up his cross and follow Me. For whoever wishes to save his life will lose it; but whoever loses his life for My sake will find it. For what will it profit a man if he gains the whole world and forfeits his soul? Or what will a man give in exchange for his soul?" (Matthew 16:24–26).

Simon, upon entering Jerusalem and minding his own business, is commandeered to go to Calvary—and witnesses what happens to Jesus. Imagine the confusion—even anger—he must have felt, but this hour of bitterness would soon turn into a blessing! Apparently, this event so marked his life that Simon the Cyrene gave his heart to the Savior whose cross he carried! Mark, whose gospel account was directed to the church at Rome and the believers there, wrote that Simon's sons were named Rufus and Alexander, implying that they were known by, and even familiar to, the believers there (15:21). This idea gains even more support in Romans 16:13 when Paul greets a man named Rufus as part of that very same Roman assembly! Paul's greeting to Rufus is warm and familial as he writes, "Greet Rufus, a choice man in the Lord, also his mother and mine." Obviously Rufus is not just a casual Christian since Paul calls him a "choice man in the Lord." And Paul feels such a closeness to him that he claims Rufus's mother as His own! Admittedly, the names Rufus and Alexander would have been common names in the first century, but there would be no reason for them to be included in the context of Mark 15 and Romans 16 if they were not known to the church of Paul's day as people of faith.

Imagine, shame turned to salvation as Christ—Simon's Savior—died on the very cross that he carried. Simon is one man, but more than that. He is a man representative of a world of people for whom Christ was voluntarily taking the cross—its shame, its penalty, and its death. Simon may have been only one man, but he was one man who had eternal significance—because Jesus not only died for the world, He died for the individual persons that make up that world.

THE WOMEN

And following Him was a large crowd of the people, and of women who were mourning and lamenting Him (Luke 23:27).

As Simon the Cyrene takes the weight of the cross of Christ on his own shoulders, the trek resumes its bloody path. Yet in all the throngs that are teeming around the little group heading for Calvary, something is missing. To be more exact, some people are missing. In another disappointing episode for the disciples, they are nowhere to be found—in spite of their bold promises not to abandon the Christ. They are in hiding, trying to understand how things that only days before were so bright and optimistic have, in a matter of hours, turned painfully bleak. Interestingly, however, while the Eleven are missing in action, the women who had served Christ faithfully were courageous in their love of the Master. While the disciples are secluded somewhere in the darkness fearing for their lives, the daughters of Jerusalem publicly mourn the suffering that Christ is so publicly enduring.

It is interesting that nowhere in the gospels is a woman ever portrayed as an enemy of Christ. In a time when women were treated as only a notch or two above cattle, Jesus treated women with dignity, respect, and tenderness. In a culture that dealt with women harshly, Christ elevated women with tenderness and honor. In a social structure that at times could be characterized by its brutality toward women, Christ reached out with kindness, and His example gave hope to women locked in a culture of hopelessness.

I was reminded of Christ's care for the hurting and suffering women of His generation when I was in Peru for a series of pastors' conferences in the fall of 2004. In the city of Huanuco (population 225,000) we collaborated with an evangelical organization named *Paz y Esperanza* (Peace and Hope), which has a ministry to the people of Huanuco—the most intensely poverty-stricken region in Peru. There, poverty has created an environment that breeds alcoholism, drug abuse, sexual abuse of children, and domestic violence against women. For the women of Huanuco, life is a degenerative cycle of fear and violence with little or no hope of escape. And, as one poet said, "There is no death so tragic as the end of hope." To these women, Peace and Hope seeks to communicate and affirm that the Christ who reached out to women in a world of danger still reaches out to the suffering women of the world today. It is a significant part of the organization's mission—and it is a marvelous reflection of the heart of the Savior.

On that day, those women of Jerusalem mourned Christ, honoring with their tears and grief the One who had honored them with goodness and warmth. Luke says that they "bewailed" him (23:27 KJV). It is an intense word that means to beat the breast in a sign of grief. They also "lamented" Him—meaning that they sang dirges, wailing in sorrow over what they saw in Him.

- **His Condition:** Beaten beyond recognition and unable even to walk normally, Jesus' physical condition should have been pathetic to even the hardest of hearts. To see anyone in that condition would have been painful, let alone the Christ who had eased the pains of so many others.
- **His Sentence:** Without question, Jesus' earthly destiny was fixed, and He would soon be affixed to a cross. The horror of death on a cross all by itself would be enough to make a normal person feel compassion for the sufferer. As we will see, it was a death intended to generate fear and horror.
- **His Humiliation:** Only days before, Jesus had triumphantly entered Jerusalem, and now He leaves the city on His way to a most violent death. The exaltations of Palm Sunday are replaced with the unbelievable anguish of the Via Dolorosa—and Golgotha in the distance.

These women respond to Jesus' suffering with a suffering of their own. And out of all the shouts and screams of the mob, Jesus hears their tears and their broken hearts. Even in His battered, condemned state, Jesus is still in control. As a result, He stops the processional and speaks to them! What does He say?

But Jesus turning to them said, "Daughters of Jerusalem, stop weeping for Me, but weep for yourselves and for your children. For behold, the days are coming when they will say, 'Blessed are the barren, and the wombs that never bore, and the breasts that never nursed.' Then they will begin TO SAY TO THE MOUNTAINS, 'FALL ON US,' AND TO THE HILLS,

'COVER US.' For if they do these things when the tree is green, what will happen when it is dry?" (Luke 23:28–31).

Don't Weep for Me

It's as if Jesus were saying to them, "I don't want your pity—I want your faith!" The entirety of the gospel is that it is rooted in a Substitute, the Christ who suffers in our place. There would be no redemption without suffering, and Christ had embraced that suffering when He embraced the cross. Now the daughters of Jerusalem need to embrace that reality as well. It is a challenge for them to move beyond the emotion of the moment to the powerful truth of what was happening there.

Weep for Yourselves

"The days are coming!" What days? Days when the world will be judged for its rebellion against God. It will be a day so intense that Jesus tells the daughters of Jerusalem three shocking things:

- **"Blessed are the barren"**—What a startling statement! Children are supposed to be a blessing, but not in that day that is to come! As strange as that statement sounds to our ears, it would have seemed unthinkable to the women of Jesus' day. In that day, women gained respect and significance in their culture through childbearing. It was their way of making a difference in a world where everything was stacked against them. For first-century women to be told "blessed are the barren" would be one of the most bizarre and counterintuitive statements that could be made. "Blessed are the fruitful" was more in line with their thinking. It was impossible to imagine what could create an age so terrifying that women would prefer barrenness to child-bearing.

- "Mountains—fall on us! Cover us!"—This is an expression of sheer terror, as people seek protection from the devastation that surrounds them. Some Bible scholars believe that this refers to a time of great judgment (see Revelation 6–19) that will engulf the earth prior to Christ's return—a time when God's judgment will be unleashed upon this planet, and the people respond with fear, but not with faith.

- "Green trees and dry"—The phrase reflects the unnatural condition of the things these women were witnessing. Christ Himself is the green tree, and, as Adam Clarke writes in his commentary, *The Gospel According to Saint Luke*,

If they spare not a tree which, by the beauty of its foliage, abundance, and excellence of its fruits, deserves to be preserved, then the tree which is dry and withered will surely be cut down. If an innocent man be put to death in the very face of justice, in opposition to all its dictates and decisions, by a people who profess to be governed and directed by Divine laws, what desolation, injustice, and oppression may not be expected, when anarchy and confusion sit in the place where judgment and justice formerly presided?

With these strong words of warning to the grieving women, Jesus tells why His suffering is taking place. He is suffering in order to rescue them and the entire world from ever needing to face God's judgment! He is suffering punishment so that they (and we) will never have to suffer it.

If nothing else, we must see here the total freedom from self-pity that Jesus had. Though making His way to the cross, where He would suffer the weight of the penalty of our sin, and though He was suffering immeasurably at that very moment, still He loved, warned, and pitied those who might reject Him. We need to see our wrongdoing just as seriously. As Stalker writes in *The Trial and Death of Jesus Christ*, "If woe and anguish fell, as they did, even on the Son of God, when He was bearing the sins of the world, what will be the portion of those who have to bear their own sins?"

And so, at last, they arrive at Calvary. But, before He is crucified we must witness one more thing.

THE MYSTERY

"They gave Him wine to drink mixed with gall; and after tasting it, He was unwilling to drink" (Matthew 27:34).

Jesus would not drink the gall! The purpose of the gall was to dull and minimize the pain of those who were suffering, in this case, the intense suffering of the crucifixion experience. In fact, this was one of the few humane elements of execution on a cross, although the inhumane goal was to try to keep the sufferer alive longer to extend his suffering. This would teach a profound lesson to the watching people who might be tempted to likewise challenge Rome's authority and laws. Yet Jesus refused this relief so that the fullest impact of the suffering He must endure as our Substitute could be realized. He had to endure the fullness of suffering, not omitting any part. He would not pay part of the price, but was determined to pay it in full. It may have been this that caused the hymn writer to pen,

I hear the Savior say,
"Thy strength indeed is small;
Child of weakness, watch and pray,
Find in Me thine all in all."
Jesus paid it all,
All to Him I owe;
Sin had left a crimson stain,
He washed it white as snow.

Jesus endured the fullness of suffering, not setting aside any of it. He went the distance in order to give Himself for us.

As we have walked this road to the cross, it is significant that we have seen four distinctly different perspectives on Christ's suffering as He made His way to Skull Hill. One of those was Christ's own perspective, and it is abundantly clear—He was obeying the eternal plan of the Father in order to love and rescue lost humanity. His was the perspective of pure love in action as He offered Himself in our place, the sacrificial Lamb that stood ready to take away the sins of the world. The Shepherd, ready to lay down His life for the sheep. The redeeming Sufferer who would bear our sins in His own body on the tree. Christ's view of the cross was as unshakable as was His devotion to His Father—and His love for us.

It is the other three perspectives that we see and wonder about. As we reflect on Christ's work on our behalf, we can probably see where, at some point in each of our lives, we have shared the perspective of each one of these groups.

- **The soldiers and the mob:** Their view of the suffering Savior was scarcely removed from bloodthirsty entertainment.

For the soldiers, at best the crucifixion was just another detail to be performed. Most of the crowd mocked, laughed, ridiculed, and verbally abused the One who was at that moment paying the penalty and taking the punishment for the very acts they were committing.

• **The daughters of Jerusalem:** They wept and mourned out of pity and compassion for a human being who was being bashed and battered before their eyes. They had hearts of sympathy but needed to have hearts of faith.

• **Simon of Cyrene:** His view was one of transformation, as he moved from shame and embarrassment to faith in the Christ and forgiveness by His grace.

It is helpful to see how those people on that day responded to the suffering Savior. The challenge that each of us faces, however, is not merely to process what His suffering meant to them. We must wrestle with the impact of what it means to us. How do I react to the thought of what Christ endured? How do I react to the truth of why He suffered? How do I respond to the One who loved me that much? We have seen how it affected them—how does it affect me?

Faithful Friend, I marvel at Your patience with us. As You saw the crowds and felt their rage, You responded with a heart of grace, and I am amazed at the strength of Your self-restraint. Likewise, I marvel, Lord, at Your ability to care for the suffering women in the midst of Your own infinitely worse suffering. May I learn to be more like You—showing patience to those who would desire to do me harm and mercy to those who hurt. Amen.

PART THREE:

SALVATION

EIGHT

THE MOCKERY OF CALVARY

I love music. Its power, emotion, beauty, and energy capture me and transport my heart in ways that no other medium of expression can quite replicate. One such moment came in 1978, not surprisingly, in a recording studio. I found myself in the main studio at Great Circle Sound in Nashville, Tennessee, having just finished participating in a lengthy edit and polish session of our collegiate vocal group's second album. Our director had just called for a much-needed break, and I was alone in the control booth with our engineer. We were mostly discussing our college album project, which was nearing completion, when the engineer said, "I want you to hear something no one has yet heard. We just wrapped production on an album by Phil Johnson, and he has written a song that is unbelievable. I am going to put it on, turn down the lights, and leave you here alone to experience this song." He did, and I sat stunned, with my eyes flooded with tears as I heard these words about the cross of Christ: "And I'm the one to blame/I caused all the pain/He gave Himself/The day He wore my crown."

I think of those words and the words in the verses that follow and of that late-night, very personal worship experience from so long ago as I, and you with me, arrive at Calvary at last. We have slowly been walking with the Savior through the events of His passion, but all along we have known that eventually we would find

143

ourselves here. Golgotha towers over the entire gospel record as the eventual and inevitable destination—but it has grown on the horizon as we have walked with Christ on the pathway of His passion. Now it is the unavoidable place that we must stop and consider as He takes our sin and our penalty, our crown and our cross.

Crucifixion was an incredibly brutal form of capital punishment. The practice had been invented hundreds of years earlier by the Carthaginians, but the Romans had made it their magnum opus, fine-tuning it and perfecting it in order to prolong the death of the condemned as long as possible—maximizing the suffering of the executed criminal and making it a powerful warning to observers. Anyone who had witnessed death on a cross would think very carefully before testing the patience of Rome and her legions. Anyone foolish enough to oppose the will of Roman law would suffer the greatest degree of agony before finally dying in misery and disgrace in a form of punishment that was truly cruel and unusual. It was the perfect form of execution for a conquering army known for its "iron heel." In fact, it was so brutal that death by crucifixion was not allowed as a form of execution for Roman citizens.

All of this, however, took on added intensity when the crucifixion took place in Israel and the condemned criminal was a Jew. The horror of the physical suffering of the cross was compounded by the stigma and spiritual curse reserved for anyone "hanged on a tree" (Deuteronomy 21:23). And this has been our destination since the beginning. To set the stage for our understanding of the cross, it would be valuable to grasp a couple of key ideas that flow from the different gospel descriptions of the events of Calvary:

- In the first three gospel records, the synoptic authors (Matthew, Mark, and Luke) present the cross of Christ as an executioner's tool of pain and humiliation.

- In the fourth gospel, John, on the other hand, portrays the cross as a throne of glory.

In fact, it was both. This will be the hour of Christ's greatest anguish, and still it will also be the event that will produce His greatest glory. In this chapter we will see the cross of Jesus Christ as portrayed by the synoptics—as an experience of horror and agony. Then, in the next chapter, we will see the crucifixion of the Son of God from the perspective of the beloved apostle—as a display of glory and power and grace. Yet even in the synoptic writers' portraits of anguished suffering, the threads of grace and love dominate the canvas of their descriptions of the event.

Of significance is the fact that none of the gospel writers ever describe the actual deed of performing a crucifixion. It is described graphically and prophetically in Psalm 22, but the gospel accounts don't describe it, perhaps because no description was necessary to the immediate audience; everyone living under the Pax Romana was painfully clear in their understanding of what death on a cross looked like. For us, living in the modern era, it is a less familiar form of violence, so it is useful (though disturbing) to see the reality of the lengths to which Christ was willing to go to redeem us— lengths that included physical, emotional, and spiritual torment.

THE TORTURE OF THE CROSS

There they crucified Him, and with Him two other men, one on either side, and Jesus in between (John 19:18).

The Torment of Being Crucified

The physical aspects of the crucifixion event were excruciating. The cross was laid on the ground and the condemned stretched upon it. Historians believe that the nails—nine to twelve inches long—were probably not driven through the palms of the hands but rather through the spaces between the small bones of the wrists. This would take the nail through the main nerve center leading to the hand and would prevent the executed individual from pulling the nail through the fleshy webbing of the hand and attempting escape—as if that were possible. The victim's feet would then be overlapped and, with knees slightly bent, forced onto a small pedestal on the cross. The reason for this will be apparent later. Once the condemned was nailed to the cross, the executioners would hoist it up with ropes and drop it into a prepared hole in the ground, a socket, where the cross would come crashing down with a thud. Once in place, the executioners would then use blocks to wedge the torture instrument securely in its socket.

It seems ridiculously obvious to say, but all of this would have been unbelievably painful. The nails would have felt like flaming pokers to the nerves and muscles of the hands and feet. The lifting would have been disorienting, perhaps even resulting in momentary vertigo. Most painful of all, however, would have been when the cross was dropped into the ground. The jolt would have resulted in a violent pulling on the victim's shoulders and elbows—which were unable to "give" under the forceful wrenching of the body. This often resulted in shoulder separations and shoulder or elbow dislocations that would have been horrific. Yet as terrifyingly brutal as all of this is, it is only the beginning. The worst is yet to come.

The Torment of Crucifixion

The unbelievable pain the victim of a crucifixion suffered was created by some sadistically brilliant elements that combined to make for an awful expression of inhumanity.

First, death by crucifixion meant ultimately death by asphyxiation. Due to the position of the arms, the chest was constricted, making it increasingly difficult for the victim to breathe. The only way the condemned was able to breathe was by pulling himself up on the nails in his wrists and pushing up off the nail through his feet and the small pedestal and thereby relieving the pressure on the chest, allowing the lungs to capture desperately needed air. However, the crucified would be able to endure the pain from the nails for only a brief time, which was precisely why the nails had been driven through the areas with the highest concentration of nerves.

Only after relaxing from the pull of the nails did relief from that pain come, but once again breathing was a virtual impossibility. The pain from the nails would be slowly exacerbated by the exposure of so many open wounds to the air and the inflammation that resulted. The beatings Christ endured would have made His back raw and tattered—exposing the battered flesh to the rough wood of the cross itself and finding those wounds irritated every time He had to push Himself up and down on the cross for breath. There was never an opportunity for rest—there was only the continual effort necessary to try to keep air in the lungs. For every breath there was a price tag of intense pain. For every relief there was the panic of the onset of suffocation.

Add to all of that the fact that doctors say there was growing internal crisis in the body of the condemned as well. Because the free circulation of blood had been hindered by the damage inflicted on so many blood vessels, more blood was going to the brain than could be returned—causing intense pressure and violent pain in the brain itself. Again, it was punishment that was cruel and unusual—and it was intended to be.

The physical suffering of crucifixion goes beyond what the civilized mind can grasp. I find myself almost needing to detach myself emotionally when I try to comprehend all of this. If not, I can't keep a clear thought about it. This would be a horrible death for the worst villain, the most ruthless criminal, the most blood-thirsty killer. It would be a horrible way to treat a rabid animal or a wild predator. Yet this treatment was inflicted on the Prince of Peace, the Lover of people's souls, the Shepherd of our hearts. It is unfathomable that the Christ should have endured such treatment, and it is unsettling to think that our sin is so vile that this was the only way it could be redeemed. Yet His physical suffering, so unimaginable, was quite possibly the least significant element of His anguish.

THE HUMILIATION OF THE CROSS

Then the soldiers, when they had crucified Jesus, took His outer garments and made four parts, a part to every soldier and also the tunic; now the tunic was seamless, woven in one piece. So they said to one another, "Let us not tear it, but cast lots for it, to decide whose it shall be"; this was to fulfill the Scripture: "THEY DIVIDED MY OUTER GARMENTS AMONG THEM, AND FOR MY CLOTHING THEY CAST LOTS" (John 19:23–24).

As shocking as it may seem, the goal of this form of punishment was not only to inflict intense physical pain. It was deemed necessary to impose as much public humiliation as possible as well. In the first century, the common attire for a Jewish man included five pieces of clothing—shoes, turban, belt, loincloth, and outer tunic. Notice that the four soldiers—the quaternion responsible for Jesus' execution—divide Jesus' garments as their spoils for performing the task. Each takes a portion of clothing, but one is left, the tunic. This implies that even the loincloth had been taken—and the crucified's last shred of human dignity with it.

In a heartbreaking fulfillment of Psalm 22, the soldiers strip Jesus naked, even of His loincloth, and then gamble for the tunic. In Psalm 22:17–18, where crucifixion was prophetically described some six hundred years before it had even been invented, David had said it would be so: "I can count all my bones. They look, they stare at me; They divide my garments among them, And for my clothing they cast lots."

"I can count all my bones"—declaring that He was exposed for all to see. Amazing—all Jesus' combined earthly wealth consisted of these poor garments, and four Roman soldiers are His heirs. They gamble for all that they can get, oblivious to the fact that mere feet away Christ was freely giving all that He had out of love—for them. It is a powerful testimony to the hardness of their hearts. These were men without feeling, without pity, without care. This scene must have left the angels of heaven staring in wonder and horror, yet these men ignore it in their greed and apathy. Isaiah had been right: "He was despised and forsaken of men . . . He was despised, and we did not esteem Him" (Isaiah 53:3).

THE SPECTACLE OF THE CROSS

And sitting down, they began to keep watch over Him there (Matthew 27:36).

The King James Version says, " And sitting down they watched Him there." In his commentary on the book of Matthew, the late Bible teacher and radio speaker J. Vernon McGee observes, "As Christ suffered on the cross, they sat down and watched Him. This is the basest of all human acts . . . Here at the cross of Calvary mankind reaches its lowest depths." Now it would seem that the horrors of crucifixion have deteriorated into a spectator sport.

Why did they sit down to watch? Some say they were simply doing their duty, that they were there to guard the scene or to prevent interference. Maybe so—but if that were the case, they would be "standing guard," not sitting down. The scene is striking. As they sit down to watch, detached and unmoved by the terrible sight of execution by crucifixion, they are watching the execution of a Man who had been found innocent! The great Bible teacher of the 1800s, Alexander Maclaren, writes in *The Gospel of St. Matthew*, "they sit solidly down and take their ease at the foot of the cross, and idly wait, with eyes that see nothing," yet they gaze upon the One whose eyes see everything. They observe Christ's suffering as those who have nothing to do with it—those who bear no responsibility for it. Yet they had put Him on the cross! These observers serve as a reminder of how easily we can be self-deceived about the implications and results of our actions. It is a reminder of how cleverly we can absolve ourselves of any responsibility for our destructive deeds.

However, it is not even possible for you to begin to honor the sacrifice of the cross in your own life until you grasp the ultimate reality that you caused it! What do you see when you look upon the Christ? Do you reckon that you (and I) put Him there? This was the only possible antidote for the deadly virus of human sin and rebellion against God. Do you see Him as Savior and Lord, or, like the soldiers, does your gaze pass by with numbness that refuses to feel the weight of His agony for us?

THE MOCKERY OF THE CROSS

And above His head they put up the charge against Him which read, "THIS IS JESUS THE KING OF THE JEWS." At that time two robbers were crucified with Him, one on the right and one on the left. And those passing by were hurling abuse at Him, wagging their heads and saying, "You who are going to destroy the temple and rebuild it in three days, save Yourself! If You are the Son of God, come down from the cross." In the same way the chief priests also, along with the scribes and elders, were mocking Him and saying, "He saved others; He cannot save Himself. He is the King of Israel; let Him now come down from the cross, and we will believe in Him. HE TRUSTS IN GOD; LET GOD RESCUE Him now, IF HE DELIGHTS IN HIM; for He said, 'I am the Son of God.'" The robbers who had been crucified with Him were also insulting Him with the same words (Matthew 27:37–44).

Author and Bible teacher Warren Wiersbe writes in *Be Loyal* that the written charge, "This is Jesus the King of the Jews," constituted the first gospel tract ever written! With that declaration of His divine identity directly before them, the crowd begins to mock Jesus as He hangs crucified between two thieves—dying *with* the very kind of people He had come to die *for*. Three groups take their turns in taunting the Son of God, and their taunts all seem to center on the claims of Christ and His apparent helplessness as He hangs on the cross.

- **Passersby**: They were probably not part of the crowd that had shouted, "Crucify Him!" The crucifixion site was at a major entry point to the city of Jerusalem, and these are people entering the city to begin their day. Yet they immediately embrace the sport of tormenting the crucified ones—with little or no sense of mercy, compassion, or pity for their suffering. It didn't matter why these men were on crosses, only that they were an easy target for the slashing tongues of the crowd.

- **Chief Priests, Scribes, Elders**: These men formed the religious establishment—an institutionalized group of leaders that had often felt the sting of Jesus' condemnation. These are supposed to be formal, professional men, yet Luke's account says that they "turned up their noses and sneered at Him"—displaying precious little dignity and no compassion (23:35). These "spiritual leaders" provide a graphic display of how sin corrupts the best of things. In *The Gospel of St. Matthew,* Maclaren says, "What is more merciful and tender than true religion? What is more merciless and malicious than hatred which calls itself religious!"

- **Thieves**: At the start of the crucifixion event, both of the thieves join in the mockery. But as the day progresses, one of the thieves will see what the crowd and the soldiers and the religious fail to see, and he will repent and believe!

This random gathering of personalities has now deteriorated into a crude and calloused mob. One Bible teacher noted that their words reduce to three clear themes:

- **They deny the power of Christ**: "You who are going to destroy the temple and rebuild it in three days, save Yourself! If You are the Son of God, come down from the cross." Notice that their words raise the critical issue, "*If* you are the Son of God," a statement that echoes Satan's words during the testings of Matthew 4:3–6. Dr. A. Carson writes in the *Expositor's Bible Commentary*, "Through the passers-by Satan was still trying to get Jesus to evade the Father's will and avoid further suffering." The crowd is working from the assumption that it is weakness that is keeping Him attached to the cross, when in actuality it was His omnipotent strength! Wonderfully, it was not nails or rope or guards that held Him there, but rather it was the invisible cords of divine love.

- **They deny the purpose of Christ:** "He saved others; He cannot save Himself." Of course their perspective was flawed at its root. It was not a matter of "cannot" but a matter of "would not." They even imply (as they had in Matthew 9:3–4) that Satan powered His miracles, for if God powered them, that God of miracles would deliver Him. Clearly, in spite of all the Old Testament prophecies and all the plain statements of Christ Himself, they still did not understand why He had come. He had nothing to prove, for He had already proven it repeatedly. The unrecognized mission of Christ was not to save Himself, but to give Himself—a mission being fulfilled before them even as they denied it. Yet there is more in their words. Their comment makes a declaration of commitment, however, that they will not be willing to honor. They say that they will believe if Jesus will come down from the cross, but in fact they would not—evidenced by the fact that they did not believe when Lazarus had been raised from the dead! No, in fact, they would not believe. Stalker writes in *The Trial and*

Death of Jesus Christ, "If Christianity were only a creed to believe, or a worship in whose celebration the aesthetic faculty might take delight, or a private path by which a man might pilgrim to heaven unnoticed, they would be delighted to believe it; but, because it means confessing Christ and bearing His reproach . . . they'll have none of it." They said they would believe if He came down, but it is precisely because He did not come down that we do believe.

- **They deny the person of Christ:** *"LET GOD RESCUE Him now, IF HE DELIGHTS IN HIM."* The chief priests mockingly quote Psalm 22, which they claimed to believe was messianic, and use its words to attack Jesus' relationship with His Father. It is as if they are declaring, "Your Father has no love for you, no concern for you, no time for you!" David spoke prophetically of Messiah's rejection, saying, "As a shattering of my bones, my adversaries revile me, while they say to me all day long, 'Where is your God?'" David prophesied about what would be most painful to the heart of the Savior. Like a sword shattering His bones, their mockery took stabs at what was most precious to the Son— His relationship with the Father.

Don't miss the fact that their perspective was skewed by unbelief and hardness of heart. What makes this so chilling is that all of their mockery was based on the truth of scriptural statements, yet their understanding was utterly void of those statements' intended meaning and significance. They looked, but never saw. They listened, but never heard. Certainly it is truth itself that the tragedy here is not just what is happening to the One dying on the cross but the pathetic condition of those who behold Him with blasphemy, unbelief, and hate. Those He loves reject the King of love.

We don't know how long this continued, but it was probably the entire first three hours of the crucifixion event. During most of these hours the Living Word is silent. But His first words are striking as they echo across the Judean hillside and reverberate off the walls of Jerusalem, "Father, forgive them!" This is the measure of the depths of divine love. He doesn't declare His innocence. He doesn't call for His deliverance. He doesn't destroy them in vengeance. The Son of God, hanging on a tree, cries in pity for poor, little man—and calls out for mercy! And even as He speaks, He is accomplishing what is necessary in order for that mercy even to be available. Once again, the love of the Savior is overwhelming to us—love we have seen in His response to His enemies, His betrayer, and His scattered sheep. This love inspired hymn writer Philip Bliss to pen:

> *Bearing shame and scoffing rude,*
> *In my place condemned He stood—*
> *Sealed my pardon with His blood:*
> *Hallelujah, what a Savior!*

I have to admit that as a kid growing up in the Presbyterian church, I never "got" hymn writer Isaac Watts when we would sing "When I Survey the Wondrous Cross." I was lost in the verbiage and the somber tone, and it just seemed like another old song that was beyond my young mind. It would be years before I would begin to see ever so faintly the gleam of wonder Watts had profoundly captured in a beautiful marriage of words and music.

Long before Mel Gibson filmed his graphically stunning and bloody portrait of crucifixion in *The Passion of the Christ*, a traveling evangelist visited the Bible college I was attending. This visit was to be a turning-point event in my own understanding of and appreciation for the cross. One evening when he was ministering to us, the evangelist began, with care and precision, to describe crucifixion in general and the events of the crucifixion of Jesus in particular with a detail I had never before been forced to face. The cross had always been presented in a way that was almost sterile and safe—not at all the dangerous and gut-wrenching thing that it was. And not at all wondrous. I listened as he poured out his heart on the suffering of Christ, and I was overwhelmed by the polar opposite realities of Christ's ultimate love and the ugliness of human hatred that were in play and, at least for me, were coming into focus for the very first time. As the evangelist described the course of events leading to the death of Christ, his words led me to a clear and definitive realization of just how evil sin is—and how evil the hearts of sinful people are. Nowhere in history do we see so clearly the capacity of the human heart for rebellion, hate, and wickedness.

Yet rising from that darkness of evil is the wondrous cross, which triumphantly proclaims to our hearts the magnitude of the love of God! To gaze upon the cross is to feast your eyes upon the pivotal point of all human history. It is to consider the most dramatic display of love the world has ever seen. It is at the same time to see how God's holiness cannot tolerate sin, and yet the Holy God loves sinners. It is to begin to reckon that all of eternity hangs on the events of that moment and to understand that in the death of Christ came heaven's greatest victory—not the defeat that misguided minds might assume it to have been. As I listened that evening, I found myself made breathless and speechless by grace, silenced by love. Finally, in the passionate words of that evangelist, I saw and felt and understood what Isaac Watts had been trying to tell me all those years I had been singing his hymn in confusion. He wrote:

When I survey the wondrous cross
On which the Prince of glory died,
My richest gain I count but loss,
And pour contempt on all my pride.

See, from His head, His hands, His feet,
Sorrow and love flow mingled down;
Did e'er such love and sorrow meet,
Or thorns compose so rich a crown?

Holy God, what a price You paid to redeem my heart!
Loving Christ, what a sacrifice You made to forgive my
sins! Precious Spirit, what a gift You gave to inhabit my
life! Teach me the joy of a heart that worships You with
this passion—"Were the whole realm of nature mine,
That were a present far too small: Love so amazing, so
divine, demands my soul, my life, my all." Dear God,
help me to know it and to live it—by the grace of Your
wonderful cross. In the name of the One who loved me
enough to take my cross, amen.

CHAPTER NINE

THE MAJESTY OF CALVARY

Christmas is the high season of the Christian faith, filled with warmth, joy, and good will. It calls us to gaze upon the Baby in the manger and know that peace is now possible, for the Prince of Peace has arrived. Filled with shepherds, a bright and shining star, and an angelic choir, Christmas is marked by light and hope. Yet hard as it is to remember sometimes, all the events of the first Christmas occurred under a shadow—the shadow of the cross. In one of my favorite Christmas carols, the hymn writer clearly understood the reality that the Christ was "Born to die, that man may live." A disturbing, powerful, glorious truth.

"Born to die." Apart from Christ, all human beings are born under a death sentence because of the disobedience of our ancient parents, but that is different. It is our penalty as fallen people. Death was not Jesus' penalty—it was His destiny. It was not His lot in life; it was His mission. It was not His unavoidable fate; it was His purpose statement for coming to the earth that first Christmas: "Born to die."

Now we have come to that awful and awesome moment when the fulfillment of mission is upon us. Now we see the Savior fulfilling the destiny that had caused Him to declare to Pilate, "For this I have been born" (John 18:37). Here, we will see what that meant.

We will draw near and see how the Son of God dies—in splendor and majesty, not in defeat and loss.

We saw in the last chapter that the gospel records give us two very different views of the cross of Jesus Christ. The Synoptic Gospels (Matthew, Mark, and Luke) describe the agony and humiliation of the cross by rightly presenting it as a tool of torture and execution. John's gospel, however, paints a very different portrait of the events of that first Good Friday. John wants us to see the cross as a throne of glory and power—a throne from which the Son of God conquers death and sin and Satan. He presents us with the unquestionable evidence of the death of the King of kings, who was to embrace His greatest glory as He embraced the cross.

As we move back into the scene before us, the crucifixion event will, in its entirety, cover about six hours. During those six hours, the gospel writers capture a series of seven sayings of Christ from the platform of the tree of death—sayings sometimes referred to as the Seven Last Words. These declarations, like the edicts of a king from his royal throne, are filled with significance but are also intentionally directional in nature.

The first three statements are horizontal in nature, describing Christ's conclusion of His dealings with the sons of men. They are statements characterized by the following:

- **Forgiveness:** "But Jesus was saying, 'Father, forgive them; for they do not know what they are doing'" (Luke 23:34).
- **Redemption:** "And He said to him, 'Truly I say to you, today you shall be with Me in Paradise'" (Luke 23:43).
- **Compassion:** "When Jesus then saw His mother, and the disciple whom He loved standing nearby, He said to His

mother, 'Woman, behold, your son!' Then He said to the disciple, 'Behold, your mother!' From that hour the disciple took her into his own household" (John 19:26–27).

Having completed His earthly tasks, the Savior now turns His attention heavenward and to the ultimate task at hand. His final four statements are vertical in nature and engage His Father in the redemptive act that is occurring on the cross of Calvary. These statements express the spiritual aspects of Christ's work as He progresses through these stages:

- **Abandonment:** "About the ninth hour Jesus cried out with a loud voice, saying, 'ELI, ELI, LAMA SABACHTHANI?' that is, 'MY GOD, MY GOD, WHY HAVE YOU FORSAKEN ME?'" (Matthew 27:46).
- **Readiness:** "After this, Jesus, knowing that all things had already been accomplished, to fulfill the Scripture, said, 'I am thirsty'" (John 19:28).
- **Fulfillment:** "Therefore when Jesus had received the sour wine, He said, 'It is finished!' And He bowed His head and gave up His spirit" (John 19:30).
- **Release:** "And Jesus, crying out with a loud voice, said, 'Father, INTO YOUR HANDS I COMMIT MY SPIRIT.' Having said this, He breathed His last" (Luke 23:46).

The charge has been placed above His head, "This is Jesus the King of the Jews" (Matthew 27:37), and everything we see here speaks of His true majesty as not only the King of the Jews, but the King of kings.

THE MAJESTY OF COMPASSION

Therefore the soldiers did these things. But standing by the cross of Jesus were His mother, and His mother's sister, Mary the wife of Clopas, and Mary Magdalene. When Jesus then saw His mother, and the disciple whom He loved standing nearby, He said to His mother, "Woman, behold, your son!" Then He said to the disciple, "Behold, your mother!" From that hour the disciple took her into his own household (John 19:25–27).

Now we see the contrast. In gambling for His clothes, the soldiers did one thing in response to the Son of Man, but the women responded very differently. Even in death, Jesus draws a line in the sand and separates people into groups based upon how they identify with Him. The soldiers are there in their greed and apathy, but the women are there out of love and devotion. Very different motives. Very different hearts. Very different agendas.

There are in fact four women present—yet apparently, in the eyes of the crowd, they are largely unnoticed. Though certainly at risk for identifying with the condemned Nazarene, they may have been able to stay under the radar simply because they were women. Their presence, however, though largely unnoticed by the crowds, was most definitely noticed by the Christ. As He gazes down from the cross, whom does He see?

- **Mary, His mother**, experiencing what Simeon had prophesied so many years before when he told her that "a sword will pierce even your own soul" (Luke 2:35).
- **Salome, Mary's sister** (Mark 15:40), apparently the wife of Zebedee and the mother of James and John (Matthew 27:56).

- **Mary, the wife of Clopas.** Some scholars maintain that Clopas was the same name as Alphaeus. If this is accurate, this Mary would have been the mother of James "the Less" (Matthew 10:3), Matthew (Mark 2:14), and perhaps even Judas (not Iscariot).
- **Mary Magdalene,** with whom we will visit more a bit later.

Their presence shows the depth of their love for Christ, and what a contrast is here! Jesus had strongly rebuked Salome (Matthew 20:22), but she was still there. Jesus had rescued the Magdalene from seven demons, and she had never forgotten His grace (Luke 8:2). Now, at what must certainly have felt like the end, they are both still at His side.

Yet as the Savior looks at these women at the foot of the cross, it is His mother who captures His heart. While His heart must have been touched by the love and devotion of the other women, His attention is focused on Mary. In *The Gospel of John*, James M. Boice cites one poet who describes Mary's love for her Son this way:

> *Near the cross her vigil keeping,*
> *Stood the mother, worn with weeping.*
> *Where He hung, the dying Lord.*
> *Through her soul, in anguish groaning,*
> *Bowed in sorrow, sighing, moaning,*
> *Passed the sharp and piercing sword.*
> *O the weight of her affliction!*
> *Hers, who won God's benediction,*
> *Hers, who bore God's Holy One:*
> *O that speechless, ceaseless yearning!*
> *O those dim eyes never turning*
> *From her wondrous, suffering Son.*

How it must have intensified His own suffering to see her in such grief. At the grave of Lazarus, Jesus had wept over the tears of Mary and Martha—how much more must He have been moved by his mother's weeping. Finally, He speaks to her—and still He is ever in control. By calling her "Woman," He severs the old relationship of mother and son. Though not a term of disrespect, it is not a term of endearment, either. It signals a shift in how they are to relate to one another. In John 2:4, He had also called her "Woman" and told her His hour had not yet come. Now that hour was here—and she needed Him to die for her sins as well!

Yet even in the dissolving of the old relationship, there is the concern of the Christ for a hurting woman. In compassion for her loneliness and loss, Jesus turns to John—the only disciple willing to stand with the women at the cross of the Master. It is apparent that Joseph is no longer living by this time, and Jesus' half-brothers do not yet believe (though they will). As a result, Christ entrusts her to one of His true family and guarantees her well-being by giving her to the disciple that He loves, John. Of this tender care and loving compassion, James Stalker writes in *The Trial and Death of Jesus Christ*, "From the pulpit of the cross, Jesus preaches a sermon to all the ages on the fifth commandment." Bible scholar William Barclay agrees, as he writes in his commentary on the gospel of John:

> There is something infinitely moving in the fact that Jesus, in the agony of the cross, when the salvation of the world hung in the balance, thought of the loneliness of His mother in the days ahead. He never forgot the duties that lay to His hand. He was Mary's eldest son, and even in the moment of His cosmic battle, He did not forget the simple things that lay near home. To the end of the day,

even on the cross, Jesus was thinking more of the sorrows of others than of His own.

That is the definition of compassion. In the midst of His intense sufferings, Jesus cares for those He loves and, in so doing, concludes His dealings with men. With Mary's care secured, His focus now shifts upward to the purpose behind it all—the awful task of becoming the Lamb of God, the sin-bearing sacrifice, for a lost human race.

THE MAJESTY OF CORRUPTION

Now from the sixth hour darkness fell upon all the land until the ninth hour. About the ninth hour Jesus cried out with a loud voice, saying, "ELI, ELI, LAMA SABACHTHANI?" that is, "MY GOD, MY GOD, WHY HAVE YOU FORSAKEN ME?" (Matthew 27:45–46).

The "sixth hour" (v. 45) represented midday—high noon. Yet, at the moment that the sun should have been at its peak, at the time when the Judean sky should have been ablaze with light, it is as if all the light of creation itself is turned off. The sky goes dark, and it is, as one songwriter put it, "midnight in the middle of the day." Something amazing is happening on the center cross—what is it? The apostle Paul would later describe the transaction in this way: "He [the Father] made Him [Christ] who knew no sin to be sin on our behalf, so that we might become the righteousness of God in Him [Christ]" (2 Corinthians 5:21).

It is what Isaiah prophesied when he wrote, "But the LORD has caused the iniquity of us all to fall on Him" (Isaiah 53:6). In that awful moment, the Priest became the Lamb. Peter comments that,

"He Himself bore our sins in His body on the cross" (1 Peter 2:24). Christ is totally engulfed by humanity's sinfulness. God chooses to lay our sins on the Lamb that is sinless and pure—and both creation and Creator respond to this awful transaction.

Nature's Response

The sky turns black because the Light of the world is now covered with our evil. All creation groans for its redemption as the earth quakes and the rocks cry out. But in and through and behind those events, God is at work. The earthquake causes the veil that guarded the Holy of Holies in the temple of Jerusalem to be torn apart, making it now possible for all who come in Christ's name to have "access through faith" (Ephesians 3:12) to the very presence of God.

All of this is happening as the Father is at work in the dark. The darkening of the sun was understood to be an emblem of mourning, and Jewish religious leaders felt such an event was somehow connected to the coming of Messiah. Yet this event is beyond natural explanation. It is not an eclipse, because it occurred during the Passover full moon. It is a darkness that is too intense to be a mere storm. The only reasonable explanation is that God did it to allow creation to mourn the death of the Creator and to prevent sinful human eyes from watching the terrible, wonderful expression of grace offered up by the Christ on the cross.

Father's Response

More than mere darkness, however, the Father's response is silence—a silence that, to the sin bearer, was received as abandonment. The death of Christ—what a thing this is. Martin Luther described this abandonment by declaring, "God, forsaken of God, who can know it?" One preacher said, "God's wrath demanded it;

God's love supplied it; God's grace presents it; God's Son secures it; God the Father allowed it." Even with the armies of heaven at His disposal, Christ submits to the eternal plan, which is nonetheless allowed to unfold uninterrupted. For this was the plan of the ages, and this was the goal of incarnation. This was why Jesus had come. And this was why the Father had sent Him.

Christ's Response

The Son of Man now responds as well, with two declarations of pain—both of which, I believe, are directed to His Father!

- **"My God, my God, why have You forsaken Me?"**: David's prophetic words in Psalm 22:1 now find flesh. The anticipation of Gethsemane has reached the horrors of reality, for the terrors of the garden have become the corruption of Calvary. The unutterable sufferings of Christ are from the Father's own hand! Isaiah 53:10 prophesies that all of this comes from the Father: "But the LORD was pleased To crush Him, putting Him to grief."

Christ cries out in terror, His rejection at the hands of men infinitely intensified by being separated from His Father—for the first time in all of eternity! The cry "My God" represents the pleading of a desperate sinner, though He had never sinned. Jesus feels the full weight of His isolation for, in the intense silence and withdrawal of His Father, Christ experiences a new thing—He is absolutely alone. "Suspended between heaven and earth, yet rejected by both." Stalker writes powerfully in *The Trial and Death of Jesus Christ* of the aloneness of the Savior in this instant:

How near He is to us! Never perhaps in His whole life did He so completely identify Himself with His poor brethren of mankind. For here He comes down to stand by our side not only when we have to encounter pain and misfortune, bereavement and death, but when we are enduring that pain that is beyond all pains, that horror in whose presence the brain reels, and faith and love, the eyes of life, are put out—the horror of a universe without God, a universe which is one hideous, tumbling, crashing mass of confusion, with no reason to guide it and no love to sustain it.

- **"I am thirsty"**: "After this, Jesus, knowing that all things had already been accomplished, to fulfill the Scripture, said, 'I am thirsty.' A jar full of sour wine was standing there; so they put a sponge full of the sour wine upon a branch of hyssop and brought it up to His mouth" (John 19:28–29). During His ministry, Jesus had often addressed the topic of thirst: "Blessed are those who . . . thirst for righteousness . . ." (Matthew 5:6); "If anyone is thirsty, let him come to Me and drink" (John 7:37); "I was thirsty, and you gave Me something to drink" (Matthew 25:35). What an irony—the Living Water crying out in thirst!

But now when He cries in thirst, a branch of hyssop is used to bring a vinegar-soaked sponge to His mouth—hyssop, the instrument used in the Passover celebration to apply the blood of the lamb to the doorposts and header of the front door of the house. But why—why does He thirst? I would suggest that He is not thirsty for water or vinegar. He is thirsty for the cup of suffering He had asked to pass by Him in the garden sufferings of Gethsemane.

But even beyond that, He thirsts for the fellowship and presence of His Father to be restored to Him! He feels the depths of the words of Psalm 42:2, "My soul thirsts for God, for the living God; When shall I come and appear before God?" If the cry of dereliction, "My God," announced the beginnings of His sin bearing, then perhaps these words represent its end. Separated by three hours, the words of the Lamb describe extraordinary longing for the Father.

Thirsty once more for the communion and fellowship of the Father, Jesus has paid the penalty—the suffering is completed. Certainly the look of horror upon the face of the abandoned Christ alone in the dark is now replaced by the calm of the Son, once more experiencing the light of the Father's presence. All that is left is to announce the victory—a victory that completely provides a solution for the problem of sin for all people of all ages.

THE MAJESTY OF COMPLETION

Therefore when Jesus had received the sour wine, He said, "It is finished!" And He bowed His head and gave up His spirit (John 19:30).

"It is finished!" In the Greek, it is "*te telestai*"; "It is completed"; "I have done it!" Matthew 27:50 says that Jesus' last words were cried with a loud voice—it is a victory shout! Cited by James Boice, Spurgeon says,

> It would need all the other words that were ever spoken to explain this one word. It is altogether immeasurable. It is high, I cannot attain to it. It is deep, I cannot fathom it!

Jesus' commitment to the Father's plan had been evidenced throughout His earthly ministry, and He has carried that commitment all the way to the end—obedient unto death, even death on a cross (Philippians 2:8): "Jesus said to them, 'My food is to do the will of Him who sent Me and to *accomplish His work*'" (John 4:34, emphasis added). "I glorified You on the earth, having *accomplished the work* which You have given Me to do" (John 17:4).

He had done it all! He left no prophecy unfulfilled, no work undone, no love unshared, no suffering unaccomplished. He had done all the Father had sent Him to do, and now He rests. But as in Genesis 2 following creation, it is not the rest of weariness Jesus experiences. It is rather the rest of completion—the rest of fulfillment. He had completed salvation—no more sacrifices were ever to be needed. No more ritual would ever need to be performed. No human effort would ever be required. As the gift of eternal grace, Jesus had completed salvation, once for all. For us.

THE MAJESTY OF CONTROL

And Jesus, crying out with a loud voice, said, "Father, INTO YOUR HANDS I COMMIT MY SPIRIT." Having said this, He breathed His last (Luke 23:46).

Notice the regal composure of the Christ. He has done what He said. He has paid for sin. He has secured redemption. He has become the ransom for suffering and death—all "for the joy set before Him" (Hebrews 12:2)! All that remains is for Him to finalize it all—by dying. Yet even here, He is in control. Notice carefully how Jesus addresses the God of heaven during these six hours of suffering on the cross. At the outset of the crucifixion, He turned to His Father in seeking pardon for sinful men. At the instant the sins of the world are placed upon Him, he cried "My God" with the derelict cry of abandonment. Now the deed is done, and again He cries, "Father." Mission accomplished. Relationship restored.

Fully aware of all that must occur, Jesus dismisses His spirit to the Father's care precisely at 3:00—the time of the afternoon sacrifice. And He dies. Yet in none of the gospel records does it *say* that He dies. He simply, purely, and powerfully fulfills His own words of purpose, words that fully showed His control when He said, "For this reason the Father loves Me, because I lay down My life so that I may take it again. No one has taken it away from Me, but I lay it down on My own initiative. I have authority to lay it down, and I have authority to take it up again. This commandment I received from My Father" (John 10:17–18). Ever submissive to the Father's love and ever obedient to the Father's will, now, at the end, Jesus commits His spirit to the Father and dies. Commentator Boice cites an anonymous poet, who writes:

> *The Head that once was crowned with thorns*
> *Is crowned with glory now;*
> *A royal diadem adorns the mighty Victor's brow!*
> *The highest place that heaven affords*
> *Is His, is His by right,*
> *The King of kings and Lord of lords, and heaven's*
> *eternal Light!*

I grew up going to church. It was just what we did. Every Sunday we were there, and every Sunday we sat (mostly) quietly and listened to things we didn't understand. Yet in all those years, I do not ever remember hearing the message of Christ explained. I never heard the gospel. Christmas was presents, and Easter was a mystery, with neither resulting in virtually any spiritual impact on my life. As I grew, I detached myself from those roots of institutional, cultural Christianity and drifted far away from the moorings of religion. It just felt incredibly empty and void of meaning or power or life. I graduated from high school and shifted churches looking for answers, finding none.

Then, in 1972, an event happened that would ever mark the path of my life. I was working for the gas company in West Virginia on a survey crew that was charged with surveying for pipelines, well locations, and a variety of other civil engineering projects. On a cold January day, we were scheduled to run a survey for a "core hole" where engineers would drill for coal—coal that could be used in experimentation for coal gasification. The survey needed to begin at a US government benchmark in order to ensure that we were starting at an accurate altitude, and the benchmark in question was on the abutment of a railroad bridge over a dry creek bed near Fort Gay, West Virginia. I climbed up to the bridge (as low man on the crew) while my colleagues enjoyed the warmth of the car. Once on the bridge, I easily found the benchmark disc implanted in the concrete of the abutment. That was when "it" happened.

I don't clearly remember how it happened, but I do remember that news reports said the winds that day were gusting into the 70-mile-per-hour range, so I have assumed all these years that a gust of wind came roaring from the hollow behind me and knocked me from the bridge. I bounced off the abutment I had been carefully studying just moments before and landed on my neck in the dry creek bed thirty-eight feet below. My coworkers hauled me from the ravine and took me to the hospital in Huntington where I spent the next week in traction—leading to three months of disability leave.

During my hospitalization, I was in a four-bed ward, and, though I couldn't turn and look because of the traction device on my neck, I knew the man in the bed next to mine was older and in bad shape. One day, as his wife was visiting him, I could hear them whispering and crying. I assumed that they had just received bad news from the doctors and were hurting over it. How wrong I was! At the end of visiting hours, the wife started to leave but stopped by my head. She looked down into my face, and I could see the tears in her eyes when she said, "My husband just told me what happened to you. We believe God spared your life because He wants to use you. We've been praying for you and will continue to pray for you."

I had never considered such a thing, but lying in a hospital bed in traction gives you a lot of time to think. In the months ahead, my searching would lead me to yet a different church—one that taught the Bible. A different job—with a Christian coworker who encouraged me in the things of Christ. And a different destination. My journey ended up in, of all places, a Christian college. There, in a chapel service on October 12, 1973, I heard the gospel explained, and I embraced the Christ of the cross as my own. He had captured my heart with His grace, and I became a follower of Christ.

I have often looked back on the path my life took and think of the emptiness of religion—but that has been resolved by the fullness of Calvary. I have thought about that dear couple in the hospital who prayed for me and their kindness and concern—but that is dwarfed by the compassion of Calvary. I have thought about that coworker who gently nudged me in the direction of the things of faith and his patience—but that is almost obliterated by the patience and loving-kindness of the holy God who looked at my sins and sent His Son to die on a cross because He was "not willing that any should perish, but that all—including me—should come to repentance" (see 2 Peter 3:9 NKJV). Now, more than forty-five years later, I value all those road markers along the way so deeply, but it is the Christ and His powerful love that have given my life the meaning and significance it never had. All of that because of the cross. All of that because, in His majesty, He came to be my Savior. The songwriter asks, "Amazing love! how can it be? / that Thou, my God, shouldst die for me?"

Precious Savior, what a powerful love You have shown us. Thank You for the glory of the cross and for the eternal purposes you accomplished there. Thank You for the way that You have opened heaven and for the privilege it is now to be called a child of God. Thank You that Your love endures forever and will never fade. Thank You for the cross of love that brings life through Your death. Thank You for enduring the cross and despising its shame. And thank You for doing it because You love me. In the power of Your cross of love I pray, amen.

TEN

THE VICTORY OF CALVARY

In the world of popular music, one of the most common themes, of course, is the pursuit of love. Surprisingly, however, popular music also addresses another significant and contrasting concept— the reality of death. On the Beatles' *Revolver* album, we hear the lament of Father MacKenzie's sad and solitary task of burying Eleanor Rigby, "wiping the dirt from his hands as he walks from the grave." In "Galveston," made popular by singer Glen Campbell, Jimmy Webb's words and music capture the fears of a young soldier in Vietnam, cleaning his gun and wondering if he will ever again see the love of his life, while crying, "I am so afraid of dying." Bob Dylan fatally accepted his own mortality when he sang, "He not busy being born is busy dying." In "I Love You This Much," country artist Jimmy Wayne sings about the funeral of a father who never loved his son but whose death is mourned nonetheless. Most recently, country superstar Tim McGraw hit the top of the charts with a song dedicated to his late father, former major-league baseball pitcher Tug McGraw, who died of brain cancer. The song title? "Live Like You Were Dying." The list could go on almost indefinitely. Like love, death is an idea that seems to stay close to the front of our minds. We fear it, struggle with it, and do all that we can to avoid and forestall it.

The Bible deals with the theme of death from a very different perspective, however, in Romans 6:23 where Paul writes, "The wages of sin is death." Death is more than just an enormous question mark. It is the ultimate reality. It entered the world because of the disobedience of our ancient parents in a garden of glory and to this day continues to hover over fallen humanity like a dark specter (the "Grim Reaper") that we cannot escape. The old saying "The only things certain are death and taxes" has stood the test of time for a reason. Death is inescapable. It is the one event in life for which there is no "Get-Out-of-Jail-Free" card. Except . . .

When Christ came into the world, it was to redeem a fallen human race. In order to do that, however, Christ had to do something pretty unimaginable—He had to kill death. He had to kill death dead. And making it even more unimaginable, Jesus had to kill death dead by dying. That was what the cross was all about. Killing death. The Son of God took sin's penalty so that the guilty could go free; the wages of sin—death—have been dealt with and resolved. The resurrection of Christ stands to declare it. We want to explore the depth of that amazing truth—and we will do that by entering into the experience of a very special woman. This woman bears witness to the victory of the cross by bearing witness to the empty tomb. And her rescue declares life and hope and victory for all of us as well. We experience the resurrection in the heart and mind of Mary Magdalene.

DEVOTED LOVE

What a brutal season of darkness the followers of Christ had experienced. From the shock of Jesus' arrest and trials to the brutality of the crucifixion to the fear that they were next—all of it had driven them into hiding. The disciples had been devastated by the events of those recent days. Their sensibilities had been shaken by the death of the Master. That is what death does—it shakes us.

In over twenty years of pastoral ministry, I have stood by the graves and the grieving families of many people. Too many, I guess. Yet it seems from those experiences that one of the things that is ever-present in episodes of grief is the hunger to *do* something. Grief demands an outlet, so we look for something to do, to show our love one final time. I felt this deeply in 1980 when my father died. People—wanting to do something to help—brought food, sent flowers, mailed cards, and offered words of comfort. Family members, especially the seven kids that had called the deceased "Dad," shared memories, attended to details of the memorial, and saw to the care of our mom. The days crawled by, and it seemed like nothing we did made any appreciable difference. Nothing could dull the pain of this deep loss, and I found myself unable to express my sorrow except to stand vigil by the casket—a silent sentinel of pain that wouldn't go away. Unable to do anything else, at least able to stand watch.

I suspect those feelings are very similar to the emotions Mary Magdalene and the other Mary (along with Salome and Joanna, the wife of Chuza, Herod's steward) must have felt as they made their way to the tomb of Jesus. Helpless to do anything but grieve, they had found a final way to express their love and devotion to the Christ. In their haste to beat the Sabbath deadline, the burial party had not ministered to the body of Jesus as thoroughly as possible. With their arms loaded with spices and embalming supplies, they left early in the morning to go to the tomb and finish the burial ceremony.

It is wonderfully appropriate that Mary of Magdala should be there. In these events, she becomes our guide and our proxy. She stands in our stead to bear witness of the events that would reshape the world. Who was she?

Her Identity

FoxNews.com reported the following story in April 2003:

Nineteen-year-old Ryan Allen was wondering why the car salesman was taking so long to check his credit. After an hour and a half, the manager of the Kansas City Chevrolet dealership came into the room with a strange question. "'Have you ever been to Yemen?' I go, "No,'" Ryan said, according to KETV-TV of Omaha. Turns out he may share a Social Security number with Ramzi Binalshibh, a Yemeni man thought to be one of the planners of the Sept. 11 terror attacks and currently being held in U.S. custody at an undisclosed location. After the April 10 discovery, the dealership called the police, who called the FBI, which refused to do anything about the matter since Binalshibh had already been arrested, Allen said. Allen didn't get his Chevy Cavalier, and a spokesman at Van Chevrolet refused to comment to the Associated Press, but that might be the least of his problems for the near future. Binalshibh—and by association, Allen as well—is on a list kept by the U.S. Treasury that orders U.S. banks to block assets of suspected terrorist financiers and enforces sanctions against some countries and suspected drug overlords.

What unfortunate consequences for that young man—all because of mistaken identity. The reputation of Mary Magdalene has also suffered greatly over the years due to a kind of "mistaken identity," but perhaps nothing has done more damage to her name than the spate of media efforts—from *The Last Temptation of Christ* to *The Da Vinci Code*—that have taken her from the role of a true worshiper of Christ to that of an alleged lover. Add to that the fact that, for years, film presentations of the life of Christ have followed traditions that presented Mary Magdalene in one way, and one way only—as a prostitute. It is important to note that there is absolutely no biblical evidence to support such a representation. This woman was much more than some kind of amoral glorified groupie. She was a true believer—and privileged beyond all others! What we *do* know of her is found in this account of her conversion in Luke 8:1–3:

> *Soon afterwards, He began going around from one city and village to another, proclaiming and preaching the kingdom of God. The twelve were with Him, and also some women who had been healed of evil spirits and sicknesses: Mary who was called Magdalene, from whom seven demons had gone out, and Joanna the wife of Chuza, Herod's steward, and Susanna, and many others who were contributing to their support out of their private means.*

What do we learn here of this Mary, called Magdalene?

- **She was of Magdala.** Some say she was called this because she was "a plaiter of hair," but it more likely is a reference to a region east of the Jordan River in the lower Galilee, an area that was probably not far from the chief city of Tiberias. Magdala is believed to have been a region with a number of villages, any of which Mary might have called home.

- **She had been demonized.** She had been possessed by no fewer than seven demons! Imagine what her life must have been like as she lived under the torment and control of these fallen angels who had possessed her body. Look at one account of the horrible life of a demoniac!

And one of the crowd answered Him, "Teacher, I brought You my son, possessed with a spirit which makes him mute; and whenever it seizes him, it slams him to the ground and he foams at the mouth, and grinds his teeth and stiffens out. I told Your disciples to cast it out, and they could not do it."

And He answered them and said, "O unbelieving generation, how long shall I be with you? How long shall I put up with you? Bring him to Me!"

They brought the boy to Him. When he saw Him, immediately the spirit threw him into a convulsion, and falling to the ground, he began rolling around and foaming at the mouth.

And He asked his father, "How long has this been happening to him?"

And he said, "From childhood. It has often thrown him both into the fire and into the water to destroy him. But if You can do anything, take pity on us and help us" (Mark 9:17–22).

- **She had been rescued.** Christ had found her in this terrible condition and had exercised the power of heaven to deal with the fallen spirits that were consuming her life. Jesus had cast those demons from her and set her free. Her life was instantly changed!

How did she respond? By becoming a devoted follower of Christ who not only talked the talk, but walked the walk. She put her money where her mouth was in support of the ministry of Christ and His disciples. Her life, values, priorities—all had been changed, radically transformed by the grace of Jesus Christ! Of course, one of the unfortunate realities we often deal with in the family of God is people who are all charged up for Christ when they first trust Him and then cool down spiritually. Would Mary of Magdala be just another casualty?

HER FAITHFULNESS

In Luke 7:47, Jesus said that the one forgiven much loves much. In the same way, I think the one rescued from the darkest pit most wondrously wants to bathe in the warmth of the light. So it is not a surprise that Mary did not want to be separated from the One who had rescued her from the depths of demonic oppression. In fact, even to the end, she was faithful when Jesus' disciples (apart from John) had abandoned Him.

She Stood by the Cross

But standing by the cross of Jesus were His mother, and His mother's sister, Mary the wife of Clopas, and Mary Magdalene (John 19:25).

No, her devotion didn't wane. Her love didn't cool. Even at the cross, heartbroken and devastated, Mary Magdalene stayed right there. Mary witnessed the brutality of the cross and the horrors of the suffering of Christ while most of the disciples were in hiding. She could not walk away. She was compelled to stay because this was where the Christ was—and she had to be with Him. While the disciples secreted themselves away, the women stayed at the scene. Watching. Suffering. Wondering. Weeping. Nothing could describe the deep sadness of their hearts at the moment Christ breathed His last from the cross of love and yielded His spirit to the Father. Yet there they were, Mary Magdalene among them. The devotion of her heart could not be set aside by the passing of time, by public opinion, by danger, or even threat of death. The hymn writer who penned these poignant words probably expresses Mary's love for Christ as well:

> *O Love that wilt not let me go,*
> *I rest my weary soul on Thee;*
> *I give thee back the life I owe,*
> *That in thine ocean depths its flow*
> *May richer, fuller be.*

The love of Christ that had redeemed Mary held her in its wonderful, devoted grip. And even at Christ's death, that love would not let her go. In his *Gospel According to John*, G. Campbell Morgan says of this love, "I never read [of this] without feeling rebuked at the loyal loving devotion of Mary Magdalene."

She Sat by the Grave

Mary Magdalene and Mary the mother of Joses were looking on to see where He was laid (Mark 15:47).

Nothing could drive Mary Magdalene and the other women from the side of their fallen Lord as Nicodemus and Joseph of Arimathea performed the grim and grisly task of removing the body of Jesus from the cross. Faithfully they followed the mournful little procession as they made their way from the Place of the Skull to the tomb—purchased by the Arimathean for his own burial but now given to the Lord he loved. Sadly they watched as the spices and wrappings were hastily applied in order to try and complete the burial before sundown—and the beginning of Shabbat. Every step of the way, these women were there. Every step of the way, their deep love for Christ overshadowed the danger of publicly identifying themselves with an executed "criminal."

Every step of the way, she was at His side—yet how tragic. She becomes to us the very image of grief. As the darkness of night deepens to match the darkness of the sorrow in her heart, Mary Magdalene sat by the grave—her heart filled with questions that had no answers.

- How could the One who commanded demons die at the hands of mere men?
- How could the One who gave her life lay lifeless in a tomb?
- How could the One who had brought light to her heart now be darkened by death?

In the darkness of gloom and grief, however, there existed the brightness of hope—hope in the One who had rescued her and redeemed her life. Even the nature of the questions calls for answers that go beyond our natural points of reference. As the hymn continues, it carries the promise of that hope.

O Joy that seekest me thro' pain,
I cannot close my heart to thee;
I trace the rainbow thro' the rain,
And feel the promise is not vain
That morn shall tearless be.

RISEN CHRIST

Now on the first day of the week Mary Magdalene came early
to the tomb, while it was still dark, and saw the stone already
taken away from the tomb (John 20:1).

Firsts are notable. Ferdinand Magellan was the first to circumnavigate the globe. Charles Lindbergh was the first to fly solo across the Atlantic Ocean. Babe Ruth was the first baseball player to hit over seven hundred home runs. Hattie McDaniel was the first African American to win an Academy Award. Neil Armstrong was the first human to walk on the moon. Tiger Woods was the first professional golfer to hold all four major titles—the Masters, the U. S. Open, the British Open, the PGA Championship—at the same time. Dr. Sally Ride was the first American woman to orbit the earth. There is something remarkably satisfying about being first—about boldly going where no one else has ever gone before.

However, Mary Magdalene is, arguably, the most significant "first" in human history! After the days of darkness, marked by the knowledge that the Lord of life was buried in a tomb, she is the first at the gravesite, and she will be the first to see the risen Savior—and we are not surprised! She comes brokenhearted, but she comes with a devotion that surpasses even the apparent certainty of death. It's important that we see that Mary had not come believing, but hurting. She had not come with a sense of anticipation, but with brokenness and grief. Yet what she lacked in understanding she made up for with love and faithfulness. And on that first resurrection morning, she would learn in a wonderful new way the truths of two Old Testament Scriptures:

- Proverbs 8:17: "I love those who love me, and those who diligently seek me will find me."
- Psalm 30:5: "Weeping may last for the night, but a shout of joy comes in the morning!"

Mary arrived at the tomb and found it empty. Fearing grave robbers, she ran to tell the disciples what she found. Then, following Peter and John, she returned to the tomb to mourn. The death she had witnessed had been disturbing; the disappearance of the body was even more distressing. Peter and John left to return to the rest of the disciples, but Mary sat at the tomb and mourned the loss of the body of Jesus—and the loss of what must have seemed like her last opportunity to serve the Savior. As she mourned, she encountered the risen Lord!

The Sound of Her Name

But Mary was standing outside the tomb weeping; and so, as she wept, she stooped and looked into the tomb; and she saw two angels in white sitting, one at the head and one at the feet, where the body of Jesus had been lying. And they said to her, "Woman, why are you weeping?" She said to them, "Because they have taken away my Lord, and I do not know where they have laid Him." When she had said this, she turned around and saw Jesus standing there, and did not know that it was

Jesus. Jesus said to her, "Woman, why are you weeping? Whom are you seeking?" Supposing Him to be the gardener, she said to Him, "Sir, if you have carried Him away, tell me where you have laid Him, and I will take Him away." Jesus said to her, "Mary!" (John 20:11–16).

It is highly significant that the risen Christ first appeared to a woman. In first-century Israel, women were generally viewed as being of low value and considered of little or no importance—but not to Christ! He valued women and treated them with a dignity and honor the world of that day would have found shocking.

Mary, brokenhearted by her loss, wept at the side of the tomb—at first oblivious to the presence of two angels! As she looked into the tomb where the body had laid, she, through her tears, saw them! Their appearance was fascinating, for they were seated at either end of the burial slab—looking very reminiscent of the Ark of the Covenant of old, where angels guarded the mercy seat! They responded to her weeping, and her only thought was that they might know where Christ had been taken. The depth of her love, measured by the depth of her grief, saw only the sorrow and loss—not the amazing reality of the angelic beings before her.

But there is more. When she turned away from them, there before her was Christ Himself! Perhaps it was her grief that blinded her eyes to His identity or perhaps, in the resurrection, Christ had the ability (as with the two disciples on the road to Emmaus in Luke 24) to mask His appearance. In any case, she assumed he was the caretaker of the burial garden and pleaded for information about the location of the body. Perhaps there was yet to be that one final opportunity to care for the One who had saved her. Little did she know.

In that most tender of moments, Jesus called her name, and she immediately recognized Him. She was shocked with joy! As Christ had taught in John 10 the Shepherd calls His sheep by name, and they know His voice. This is the Shepherd calling His sheep by name—tenderly, but with the authority of One who has conquered death. Powerfully, lovingly, gently, He says her name as it has never been spoken before: "Mary!"

The Sight of Her Lord

She turned and said to Him in Hebrew, "Rabboni!" (which means, Teacher) (John 20:16).

She faced Him, and as she saw Him, she turned from death to life; from grief to joy; from despair to belief.

She responded, "Rabboni"—teacher, master, the equivalent of "my dear Lord," the title only a believer can utter about the Christ. Her emotional roller coaster had settled in peaceful calm. She had seen Jesus alive. Mary of Magdala, once demon-possessed but now set free, once grieving but now joyful, was the first person to see the risen Christ! For the first time in days, darkness had been overwhelmed by light. Death had been killed dead by the resurrection of Christ.

DESPERATE JOY

I was on Kanawha Terrace in St. Albans, West Virginia—my boyhood home. It was late afternoon, and I had been collecting for my paper route, my tenth-grade job. I had just stopped at the Sunoco station on the corner of Kanawha Terrace and Walnut Street and was enjoying the fruit of my labors—an ice-cold Pepsi. As I stood at the corner, I heard a growing roar, and as I turned, a flash went past me and I turned to see a fairly out-of-date Oldsmobile speed through the red light at the corner. Going at least eighty miles per hour in a thirty-five-mile-per-hour zone, the car flew down the street. One block later, another car pulled out of the side street, and the two cars collided in a huge crash. Bodies went flying in all directions, and I ran to see if everyone was okay. They weren't. Two people were killed and seven hospitalized. To this day, it was the worst wreck I have ever seen. As it turns out, I was the only eyewitness to the accident, and I spent the next weeks as a fifteen-year-old kid giving depositions to lawyers and insurance representatives. They asked me a million questions, and I told them what I saw and how it felt.

That is what a witness does. Witnesses simply state the facts of what they saw and how it felt. Interestingly, the Greek word for witness is *marturos*—from which we get the word *martyr*. Why? Because Stephen was martyred as a result of witnessing about what he had seen and felt as a result of faith in Messiah Yeshua—Jesus Christ. Events in history are viewed as credible or falsified based on the integrity and character of the witnesses, and on this day, it is a wonderful blessing to know that the resurrection of Christ has many witnesses! In fact, over five hundred people saw the risen Christ at one time in only one of several post-resurrection events. The testimony of those witnesses and others, as well as the witness of two thousand years of changed lives, still declares that Jesus Christ is risen. Mary Magdalene was but one of those witnesses—but, once more, she was the first: "Mary Magdalene came, announcing to the disciples, 'I have seen the Lord,' and that He had said these things to her" (John 20:18).

Not only was she the first to see, she was the first to tell. Mary Magdalene was richly privileged because she deeply loved. And she ran back to the disciples and did what we are now to do—she told what she saw, and she told how it felt. He is alive, and because of that we have life forevermore! Joy has come where weeping had endured, for Jesus was—and is yet today—alive! For two thousand years, men, women, boys, and girls have stood up—for many of them on pain of death—to be witnesses for Christ. We are invited to join them in this grand, eternity-transforming enterprise of telling people of the risen Christ. Like Mary, our call is to go into the world and tell them what has happened in our lives because Jesus conquered death. Like Mary, we are not called to eloquence, brilliance, or cleverness. We are called to tell what has happened and how it felt.

In the movie *Meet Joe Black*, Death comes to life (an odd phrase, don't you think?) in order to, simply put, try to understand what the big deal is all about. He compels a man with a potentially fatal heart condition to instruct and mentor him in life, to understand why human beings cling to life with every ounce of strength they have. In the end, the character that represents Death discovers love and life and realizes the power that life has—but he nevertheless returns to being Death—a taker rather than a giver of life.

When Jesus Christ came into the world, He declared that His mission statement was not about death but about life! Hear His words:

- "The thief comes only to steal and kill and destroy; I came that they may have *life*, and have it abundantly" (John 10:10, emphasis added).

- "I am the resurrection and the *life*; he who believes in Me will live even if he dies, and everyone who lives and believes in Me will never die" (John 11:25–26, emphasis added).
- "I am the way, and the truth, and the *life*; no one comes to the Father but through Me" (John 14:6, emphasis added).

The Christ kept His Word and provided the rescue He had promised. In fulfilling His mission, He did the impossible by taking dead people and making them living persons. This is the victory of Calvary. The victory of love and the victory of life-changing grace is secured and made possible by the love that holds us in its arms and won't let go.

It was George Matheson who wrote the hymn "O Love That Wilt Not Let Me Go." Of his hymn of devotion, Matheson wrote:

My hymn was composed in the manse of Innelan (Argyleshire, Scotland) on the evening of the 6th of June, 1882, when I was 40 years of age. I was alone in the manse at that time. It was the night of my sister's marriage, and the rest of the family were staying overnight in Glasgow. Something happened to me, which was known only to myself, and which caused me the most severe mental suffering. The hymn was the fruit of that suffering. It was the quickest bit of work I ever did in my life. I had the impression of having it dictated to me by some inward voice rather than of working it out myself. I am quite sure that the whole work was completed in five minutes, and equally sure that it never received at my hands any retouching or correction. I have no natural gift of rhythm. All the other verses I have ever written are manufactured articles; this came like a dayspring from on high.

That is the heart of George Matheson, and it is the heart of Mary of Magdalene as well. Her identity may have been misrepresented over the years, but her witness is clear, and her devotion is unmistakable. It is a declaration of the glory of the cross and the power of the resurrection. It is the wonder of the Christ and what He does to change one single, individual, eternal life. And that is the pulse of the powerful witness Mary gives of the Savior who died and rose again that we could have forgiveness and life. Matheson's hymn ends:

> *O Cross that liftest up my head,*
> *I dare not ask to fly from thee;*
> *I lay in dust life's glory dead,*
> *And from the ground there blossoms red*
> *Life that shall endless be.*

"Life that shall endless be." Not death—life. May we, like Mary Magdalene, go forth to be living witnesses of the living Lord Jesus Christ who killed death dead so we could live life alive.

Lord of life, I thank You for Your victory—and for making Your victory my victory. I praise You for life-giving power that can only be measured by the stretch of eternity, yet can only be comprehended by the tiny sanctuary of the human heart. I rejoice in the privilege of life and celebrate in Your presence the marvelous truth that the Christ who is alive forevermore has killed death. Give me courage to live in that life, to walk in that love, and to tell. Give me courage to let others know. In the grace of Christ I pray, amen.

PART FOUR:

EXALTATION

ELEVEN

THE RETURN TO
THE FATHER

In *The Wizard of Oz,* Dorothy was right. As she clicked together the heels of the ruby slippers and closed her eyes in expectancy, she chanted softly, "There's no place like home! There's no place like home! There's no place like home!" She was right. There really is no place like home. As I write this, I am in Australia preparing to teach tonight in a Bible conference in Brisbane, Queensland. There are two colleagues from our ministry's Singapore office with me, and we have met wonderful people who have welcomed us warmly, opened their homes to us, and fed us in a spectacular way. It is comfortable, relaxed, and even mostly restful—but there is no place like home.

In 1995, I traveled internationally for the first time to Moscow, Russia, to teach pastors in a Bible institute there and was apprehensive to say the least. As a child of the Cold War, I had adopted certain presuppositions about Russians, most of them negative. With fear and trepidation I stepped off the plane and onto the jetway at Moscow's Sheremetyevo II airport, and the first person I saw was a stern-looking Russian soldier holding an AK-47 machine gun. Driving through the dark streets of Moscow with two men I had never met who did not speak English was disorienting to say the least. The next two weeks were a blur of uncomfortable adjustments that kept me off balance the entire time. I was able to learn and flex a little as we went along, but it was difficult.

Then, at the conclusion of the class sessions, we were joined by Bob Provost of Slavic Gospel Association and hopped on an Aeroflot flight (which may be the definition of *terrifying*) and flew to the southern Caucasus region near Chechnya in order to provide humanitarian aid relief to Chechen war refugees. Talk about leaving the frying pan for the fire. I really understood for the first time what it meant to be "a stranger in a strange land." We met with tragic cases of entire families—for example, twenty-seven family members in one house, all women and children—who had no idea whether any of the men of their family were even still alive. We saw mothers desperately wondering how to feed their children and wives desperately fearful of the fate their husbands may have met. It was long, tiring, stressful, and really tough to watch—and, it goes without saying, that it was much tougher on those families than it was on us. Like me, all they wanted was to go home.

As the days stretched on, I really felt the gravity of all I was witnessing. But I increasingly felt the weight of loneliness as well. I had never been away from my wife more than eight days—and that to attend pastors' conferences in the States. Three weeks felt like the death penalty. The loneliness seemed as if it would never end. Don't get me wrong—the ministry was great and the experiences rich, and, once I got over the shock of being in Russia, the people were absolutely fabulous. But there's no place like home. When we landed back in the States, I had to fight the overwhelming urge to get down on my hands and knees and kiss the ground. Back on American soil and in the same time zone as my wife and family. Home.

There's no place like home. And after more than thirty years of being physically separated from the Father during His incarnation, Christ would be returning home—to the glories of heaven.

BACKGROUND FROM LUKE

The first account I composed, Theophilus, about all that Jesus began to do and teach, until the day when He was taken up to heaven, after He had by the Holy Spirit given orders to the apostles whom He had chosen. To these He also presented Himself alive after His suffering, by many convincing proofs, appearing to them over a period of forty days and speaking of the things concerning the kingdom of God (Acts 1:1–3).

Sometimes we forget that much of the New Testament was originally written, not as historical treatises or theological creeds, but as personal letters. These writings were intended to express the author's experiences with Christ and the truth about Him. None of that diminishes the reality of inspiration in the giving of the Scriptures, but it helps us to understand the intent of the writers. They were sharing their hearts with people or churches that they cared for deeply. And this was true of both of the books credited to the dear physician, Luke.

As Luke sought to capture the events of the life of Christ and the birth of the church, he was doing so for his friend, Theophilus. In the very least, these accounts were intended to be instructional and, at the very most, evangelistic. In fact, it is likely that Luke put pen to paper (or parchment) for the express desire of seeking to reach the heart of someone he was deeply concerned for—and the millions who have comprised the body of Christ have benefited for two thousand years because Luke was concerned for one man.

In his gospel record, Luke, as we have seen, has tried to present to his friend the powerful story of the Son of Man who came to redeem the sons of men. In Acts, he shares the continuing saga of God's ongoing work in the world. It is helpful to notice that, though usually referred to as the Acts of the Apostles, the book is more accurately a telling of the acts of the Holy Spirit! It is in the coming of the Spirit that the promise of Christ is fulfilled (see John 14, 16), that the church is born, that the spread of the gospel reaches to the far corners of the world, and that the Gentile community is first brought into the embrace of the Christ. None of those things would have been even remotely possible apart from the presence and power of the third person of the Godhead.

As to the events themselves, Luke opens his letter to Theophilus with a reminder of when they happened in time and space. We reenter the story during the post-resurrection ministry of Jesus Christ. From the resurrection to the ascension was a forty-day season of Christ's continuing ministry and instruction to His followers. It was a vital time of preparation that anticipated the great work that was about to be launched. Following that forty days would be another ten days of prayer and expectation, until the day of Pentecost—and the coming of the Spirit. What happened during those forty days? No fewer than thirteen distinct, physical appearances of the risen Savior—including at the tomb, in the upper room, on the Emmaus road, in Galilee, and privately to individuals (as recorded by Paul in 1 Corinthians 15). As He met with them, he confirmed His resurrection, His victory, and His authority. It would be pretty hard to contain the joy and celebration of the followers of Christ in seeing their Master alive once more!

It would be more than appearances, however, that would mark these events. Christ continued His instruction of His disciples by teaching, particularly instructing them about the "things of the kingdom of God" (v. 3). What is that? I think it may have included two significant concepts.

- **The Kingdom on Earth**—In some significant schemes developed to understand the prophetic literature of the New Testament, the kingdom is seen as the literal fulfillment of God's promises to His people Israel. One day the kingdom will be restored, and David's greater Son—Messiah Christ—will rule and reign on the throne of God in Jerusalem for a period of one thousand years. In that era, the golden age of Solomon will be restored, and the "kingdom of the world [will] become the kingdom of our Lord and of His Christ"(Revelation 11:15). Christ will then physically reign upon the earth as King over all kings and Lord over all lords.

- **The Kingdom of Hearts**—In a more personal sense, however, is the reality that in every heart that is truly converted, Christ rules as King. This is the essence of Paul's words in Romans 14:16–17 where we read, "Therefore do not let what is for you a good thing be spoken of as evil; for the kingdom of God is not eating and drinking, but righteousness and peace and joy in the Holy Spirit." The kingdom of God ruling in the hearts of His people produces significant spiritual fruit.

Paul shows that these two kingdom concepts are related, because the rule of Christ over our hearts *now* is indicative of the rule that He will bring to the earth *then*—in His perfect timing. It is no wonder that the model prayer Christ gives to us in Matthew 6:10 encourages us to pray to the Father, "Your kingdom come.

Your will be done, On earth as it is in heaven." The Father's kingdom will physically come, and the people of the world must face this reality as they examine the claims of Christ upon their hearts. He calls us, His children, to live out those claims now, as Christ makes us kingdom people and His ambassadors and representatives on this foreign soil—until He comes to rule.

SENDING OF THE SPIRIT

Gathering them together, He commanded them not to leave Jerusalem, but to wait for what the Father had promised, "Which," He said, "you heard of from Me; for John baptized with water, but you will be baptized with the Holy Spirit not many days from now" (Acts 1:4–5).

One of the most controversial areas in all of Christian belief has to do with the role of the Holy Spirit. From Pentecostals to fundamentalists, from moderate evangelicals to mainline denominationalists, everyone has a perspective on the Spirit. The debate has particularly raged over the last thirty years due to the spread of the charismatic movement. This is not a book on the Holy Spirit, so we don't want to digress into a lengthy discussion of all these views and their respective merits and flaws. What we do want to focus on, however, is the big picture. The main idea still needs to be the main idea, even as we continue to dialogue about the issues and perspectives that undergird (or undermine) the main idea. What is the main idea?

I think the main idea was fairly clear to Luke, and the context of this passage unveils it for us. Jesus has been instructing His followers on the value and nature of kingdom living in a fallen world. As part of that, He has emphasized the significant responsibility that is ours to represent Him accurately to that fallen world. The fly in the buttermilk, however, is that we are not adequate to fulfill that challenge. We are not strong enough, smart enough, wise enough, disciplined enough, consistent enough, or godly enough. Left to ourselves, we will fail miserably in the challenge of kingdom living—and it is with that understanding that we must read Jesus' words to the disciples! Christ Himself answers our inadequacy in the promise of the Spirit—for He will be our enabling and empowering in this great adventure. The big picture of the Spirit's coming calls us to see our insufficiency, so that we will rest in the strength of His sufficiency. And even as Jesus tells them of this powerful resource, He desires to train them to be dependent upon His strength. He builds this theme two ways.

The Charge to Wait

Gathering them together, He commanded them not to leave Jerusalem, but to wait for what the Father had promised (Acts 1:4).

So, right from the start, I am frustrated. Like many in my generation, I am terribly impatient. I feel it in almost every arena of life—in traffic, on the golf course, in the drive-through at Arby's, in an airport. Waiting is one of the elements of life that is a struggle. Being told to wait feels suffocating and pointless, a result usually attached to someone else's lack of planning or preparation. For me, waiting is one of the most unpleasant experiences of life. It is easy to replace simple waiting with drive or ambition or initiative—all of which are exceedingly appropriate in the right time and place. But, as a general rule, waiting is just plain hard—unless I have temporarily put life on hold because of something that is really worth waiting for.

I remember standing at the front of a church waiting for the doors of the sanctuary to open so that my bride could enter and join me in making promises and exchanging rings. Or waiting in a room bearing the actual name "Waiting Room"—waiting for the doctor to come out and tell me our son was born. So just maybe there are moments in life when waiting is the best and most important thing we can do. The Old Testament prophet Isaiah unquestionably believed this to be true: "Yet those who wait for the LORD will gain new strength; They will mount up with wings like eagles, they will run and not get tired, they will walk and not become weary (Isaiah 40:31).

Certainly this was true of the command to wait that the followers of Jesus were given by their Lord. Their season of waiting was a time of preparation and purpose, a time of anticipation and aspiration. It was the time in which Jesus' upper-room promise would finally come true—the Holy Spirit that had been dwelling *with* believers would now actually and literally take up residence *in* believers. The result of that indwelling? Power from on high—power for living! Our Lord instructed them to wait for the coming of the Holy Spirit, but the great news for us is that we do not have to wait. If you know Christ, the Spirit is already dwelling in your life. In fact, Romans 8:9 clearly states that if the Holy Spirit is *not* indwelling your life, you are not Christ's.

We should also keep in mind, however, that though we don't have to wait to receive the Spirit, learning to wait is still a valuable and important exercise. We must learn to wait on the Lord because we sometimes need the training and discipline that such waiting can teach. Mostly, though, we need to learn to wait upon the Lord so that we can learn to rest in His always-perfect timing. One of the most useful spiritual lessons we can learn is the fact that God is always exactly on time—never early, never late. That may frustrate us, but it doesn't frustrate Him! He is completely comfortable with the perfect timing of His plans and purposes, and we can learn to be comfortable with His wise ways as well.

Notice that in Acts 1:5, Jesus tells the disciples that the Spirit would come "not many days from now." One preacher I heard noted that Jesus was fully aware that the Spirit would come in ten days (not nine or eleven) and in fact, He could have told them that. It is likely, however, that had they been told ten days, they would have gone about their own business for the first nine and then become obedient, sliding in under the tag at the last possible moment. They needed to wait upon the Lord and His will and His timing. Our Lord knows us very well—well enough to know that if we had all the information, we would never rest ourselves in Him. We would not walk with Him as we should if we knew all that we wanted to know. Sometimes we need the joy and exhilaration, the anticipation and trust that come from not knowing all the details in advance!

The Ministry of the Spirit

It is vital to see all that God's Spirit can do on our behalf that we could never do in our own effort. His work is a comprehensive expression of God's perfect care for His redeemed child. Notice all that the Spirit does for the believer:

- **He assures us of our salvation**: "The Spirit Himself testifies with our spirit that we are children of God" (Romans 8:16).
- **He equips us for spiritual service**: "But one and the same Spirit works all these things, distributing to each one individually just as He wills" (1 Corinthians 12:11).

- **He gives us power to live as witnesses:** "But you will receive power when the Holy Spirit has come upon you; and you shall be My witnesses both in Jerusalem, and in all Judea and Samaria, and even to the remotest part of the earth" (Acts 1:8).

- **He makes us capable of receiving the Word of God:** "But when He, the Spirit of truth, comes, He will guide you into all the truth; for He will not speak on His own initiative, but whatever He hears, He will speak; and He will disclose to you what is to come" (John 16:13).

- **He is our resource for living the Christian life successfully:** "So then do not be foolish, but understand what the will of the Lord is. And do not get drunk with wine, for that is dissipation, but be filled with the Spirit" (Ephesians 5:17–18).

This last statement is critical to our Christian experience, for it is in the "filling" of the Spirit that we find the day-to-day victory of life. The only way that we can live for Christ is if the Spirit is in control, filling our hearts and lives like the wind fills a sail and drives a ship. This is why Jesus had told His men in the upper room that it was profitable for them if He went away, for in His departure He would send the Holy Spirit to be the Comforter they needed—the Comforter who had been with them, now living in them. Living in us! The Holy Spirit provides all that we need and wonderfully fulfills Christ's promises to His children.

AREAS FOR CONCERN

So when they had come together, they were asking Him, saying, "Lord, is it at this time You are restoring the kingdom to Israel?" He said to them, "It is not for you to know times or

*epochs which the Father has fixed by His own authority; but
you will receive power when the Holy Spirit has come upon
you; and you shall be My witnesses both in Jerusalem, and in
all Judea and Samaria, and even to the remotest part of the
earth" (Acts 1:6–8).*

It was my privilege to spend over twenty years in pastoral ministry, serving churches in three different states and three different regions of the country. In those churches, there was as much diversity as the body of Christ itself. We had people from all levels of social strata, from a diversity of occupational backgrounds, from a wide range of educational advancement, from a variety of generations, and from a spectrum of ethnic heritages. We had people who were single, people who were married, people who had suffered the pain of divorce, and people who had celebrated more than sixty years of marital bliss together. We had people who did not yet know Christ, new believers, growing young servants of Christ, and seasoned spiritual "veterans." We had laypeople who had never been able to summon the courage to speak a word for Christ and pastors who had retired after decades of effective ministry. In a sense, it has been my privilege to minister to people of every tribe, tongue, and nation.

Yet with the myriads of things that made these people different, there were many things that they had in common, including the love of Christ and a hunger for the Scriptures. In the midst of that, though, was another common thread that may be the essence of what makes pastoral ministry so challenging. After any given worship time, having poured out my heart in trying to faithfully present God's Word, I walked away without any means to accurately measure what they heard. Now don't get me wrong—I know completely what I *said*. I just don't know what they *heard*. For all their diversity, people have at least one thing in common—they hear things, including the teaching of the Bible, through the filters of their own experience, be it good or bad. One person's joke is another's heartache. Something that may seem perfectly clear to one listener may be frustrating and confusing to another. We bring our own agendas, intentions, and life situations to the event and listen in that context.

The disciples were no different. After all that had happened and all that Jesus had said, done, and accomplished, these eleven followers of Christ were still unclear about the point of it all. In verse 6, when they ask, "Lord, is it at this time You are restoring the kingdom to Israel," it reveals they are still far from where they need to be. They are still intrigued by a desire for royalty and power and have not yet fully understood the priority of servanthood and ministry. They were hearing Jesus' teaching on the kingdom very differently from what He was saying about it!

Perhaps at the heart of the concern was the misunderstanding that considers God's blessings to be rights, not privileges. In fact, the privilege of spiritual service is even more—it is a privilege that carries with it serious responsibilities. Yet after more than three years of Christ's teaching and example, His testimony before Pilate, His cross and resurrection, and forty more days of post-resurrection ministry, the disciples are still foggy in their thinking. They are still consumed with externals, and Jesus is still seeking to draw them to consider the internals. They are concerned about their plans and timetables and need to embrace God's purposes for them—and for the world. But they would have to embrace God's purposes, for it would be their privilege and responsibility to reach out to the world with the gospel—of being those who would be accused of "turning the world upside down!" In the midst of their confusion, the Master brings clarity and outlines their mission and purpose—and the source of the power to accomplish it.

The Believer's Mission

Jesus handed His followers—the spiritual ancestors of us all—the baton of mission with words of great significance when He said, "But you will receive power when the Holy Spirit has come upon you; and you shall be My witnesses both in Jerusalem, and in all Judea and Samaria, and even to the remotest part of the earth" (Acts 1:8). That baton, like a relay race in the Olympics, has been passed down for two millennia, and we now have that mission as our own. In fact, the mission statement for world evangelism is brilliant in its lack of complexity. It answers all the key questions that "enquiring minds want to know."

- **WHO?** You!
- **WHAT?** Be My (Jesus') witnesses.
- **WHERE?** Even to the remotest parts of the earth.
- **WHEN?** Even to the end of the age.
- **HOW?** In the power of the Holy Spirit.

Believers were to begin at their own homes, then spread to the region surrounding them, to neighboring countries, and then the entirety of planet Earth. No corner of the globe was to escape their influence and message of witness. One teacher cited several key ingredients to this mission, however, and they are ingredients that we cannot ignore or overlook:

- This mission can be accomplished only in the Spirit's power. It is not dependent upon our glibness, cleverness, or talent.
- Our witness is to compel people to embrace Christ—not attempt to force their decision. It is reported that Stanley said of Livingstone, "If I had been with him any longer, I

would have been compelled to become a Christian, and yet, he never spoke to me of it at all!"

- What we are conditions what we say. Jesus commanded that we "be" His witnesses—which implies a quality of life that supports and promotes the message. Merely saying the right words, without the life of Christ in us to back it up, is not true spiritual witness.

- Our attitude and motivation as we launch into this mission is not one of guilt or obligation, of mere duty or task. Though accountable to Christ, we echo the heart of Paul who said, "For the love of Christ controls us, having concluded this, that one died for all, therefore all died" (2 Corinthians 5:14).

We are to be concerned about telling what we live and living what we tell—for the strongest witness imaginable in the purposes of God is the evidence of Christ's impact in changing our own lives! More than miracles, more than power plays, more than eloquence, the portrait of transformed hearts is powerful and irrefutable, a most formidable weapon in the hands of the Holy Spirit.

PROMISE IN THE CLOUDS

And after He had said these things, He was lifted up while they were looking on, and a cloud received Him out of their sight. And as they were gazing intently into the sky while He was going, behold, two men in white clothing stood beside them. They also said, "Men of Galilee, why do you stand looking into the sky? This Jesus, who has been taken up from you into heaven, will come in just the same way as you have watched Him go into heaven" (Acts 1:9–11).

Without question, the ascension is one of the most overlooked events in the life of Christ. While we have over the years rightly focused on Christmas, Good Friday, Easter, and the dozens of powerful events that took place in the midst of them, the ascension is set aside—for some reason not quite compelling enough to deserve our wonder. It is "only" Christ's ascending bodily into the sky in the presence of angels and before the very eyes of His followers. It is "only" the ascension—the ascension that, rightly understood, is one of the most astounding events in all the Scriptures! In fact, the ascension of Christ is the key to our hope.

Picture this amazing scene. Jesus is in the midst of commissioning His followers in the spread of the message of Calvary—and suddenly He begins to float upward! What a shock this must have been for the disciples. Yet, what a great privilege. They had not been eyewitnesses to the actual event when He rose from the grave, but they were there on the Mount of Olives to see Him rise from the earth and ascend to the presence of the Father. The scene must have been breathtaking in its quiet, awesome, overwhelming power. The sight apparently stunned the quibbling disciples into silence. Once again, Jesus had done in their presence something of which mere humans are not capable. They had seen Him walk on water. They had seen Him quiet storms. They had seen Him feed multitudes, heal sufferers, rescue demoniacs, and raise the dead. Now they watched—speechless—as He defied gravity and was whisked from their sight as they stared at the sky. It makes me wonder why we have never thought of this event as being impressive enough!

Several elements in this event, however, are in need of being underscored. These are the keys to the ascension that help us try to get our minds around such a fascinating event.

The Significance of Ascension

The ascension of Jesus validated His earthly claims as His Father receives Him. As Christ ascends, one phase of His ministry ends and another begins. His ministry had begun with creation and continued with the successfully completed purchase of salvation. Now Jesus, at the Father's side, would begin His ministry of intercession (see Romans 8:34 and Hebrews 7:25) on our behalf—to be followed one day by His coronation as King over kings and Lord over lords! In the meantime, He departs in order to fulfill His promise in sending the Spirit (John 14–16) to minister to us, in us, and through us.

The Response of the Eleven

As they watch, Jesus rises from the earth and into the sky, until He is swept from their sight by a cloud—which some have speculated to be the return of the *shekinah* glory that was present at the dedication of the tabernacle so long ago (Exodus 40:34). As He vanishes from their sight, they just keep staring up! It is likely that they kept looking up because they expected Him to return—after all, He had been leaving and returning for forty days now since the resurrection. He had always come back, but this time He didn't. This must have created a variety of intense emotions. They were surely amazed at what they had just witnessed. Perhaps they had some residual disappointment in the lack of an immediate kingdom. There may have even been an element of fear because Jesus was now really gone. To say the least, it was a watershed moment for the Eleven. They must have wondered, "What do we do now? Where do we go from here?"

The Promise of Return

As they "gazed intently" into the skies, two angels (described by Luke in Acts 1:10 as "men in white clothing") appeared and gave them significant new information. Yes, Jesus will return—but, like the kingdom, it will not be according to their timetable or agenda but in fulfillment of God's divine calendar. The emphasis, however, in the angelic message was not *when* Jesus would return, but *how!* The reality of His return would be:

- **Personal:** "This Jesus"—and not a substitute. He Himself will come again, as He had promised them in the upper room the night before the cross. He had said in John 14:3, "If I go and prepare a place for you, I will come again and receive you to Myself, that where I am, *there* you may be also" (emphasis added).
- **Powerful:** In the same way He departed, Christ will return. He left the earth and went up into the clouds and will return that same way! In the clouds and to the earth, and in that day He will answer their questions about the kingdom—for He will reign! It is the magnificent scene pictured in Revelation 19 when Christ comes with His saints, and the kingdoms of this world become the kingdoms of our God and of His Christ.
- **Practical:** The implication of this message of hope is that He is coming. Our concern is not when it will occur but rather that we be busy and faithful in serving Him while we wait. As Paul wrote, "Therefore, my beloved brethren, be steadfast, immovable, always abounding in the work of the Lord, knowing that your toil is not in vain in the Lord (1 Corinthians 15:58).

- **Purifying**: The realization that Christ could return at any moment should motivate us to live in a manner pleasing to Him! As the beloved disciple, John, wrote,

See how great a love the Father has bestowed on us, that we would be called children of God; and such we are. For this reason the world does not know us, because it did not know Him. Beloved, now we are children of God, and it has not appeared as yet what we will be. We know that when He appears, we will be like Him, because we will see Him just as He is. And everyone who has this hope fixed on Him purifies himself, just as He is pure (1 John 3:1–3).

The ascension of Jesus Christ points our hearts upward with hope and confidence! His return to the Father prepares the way for our eternal home and for His imminent return! His powerful display and the angelic explanation combine to rescue our hearts from fear and to fill our minds with His promise—He will return!

As Christ returned to the Father, He was going home—but, at least in part, He was going home to prepare a new and eternal home for us! Remember again His words in the upper room:

Do not let your heart be troubled; believe in God, believe also in Me. In My Father's house are many dwelling places; if it were not so, I would have told you; for I go to prepare a place for you. If I go and prepare a place for you, I will come again and receive you to Myself, that where I am, there you may be also (John 14:1–3).

A dwelling place in heaven for me! What a fabulous thought that is. In this world we are homeless, like Moses, who felt himself to be a "stranger in a strange land" (Exodus 2:22 KJV). In Christ, however, we are now members of His family, with this powerful result:

So then you are no longer strangers and aliens, but you are fellow citizens with the saints, and are of God's household, having been built on the foundation of the apostles and prophets, Christ Jesus Himself being the corner stone, in whom the whole building, being fitted together, is growing into a holy temple in the Lord, in whom you also are being built together into a dwelling of God in the Spirit (Ephesians 2:19–22).

To finally be home. With Him. In the presence of the Father. Forgiven, restored, accepted, and alive forever. This is why Jesus came and walked the path of the passion—for the joy awaiting Him. He came to save us and give us a home where we would never be orphaned, never be unloved, and never be forgotten. Reunion with loved ones and the splendor of heavenly eternity—wonderful as they will be—are only the whipped cream on the sundae, however. Hymn writer Charles Gabriel captured the wonders of heaven in a single verse:

When all my labors and trials are o'er,
And I am safe on that beautiful shore,
Just to be near the dear Lord I adore,
Will thro' the ages be glory for me.
O that will be glory for me,
Glory for me, glory for me;
When by His grace I shall look on His face,

That will be glory, be glory for me.

Home. At last. Forever. That will be glory!

Coming Christ, how grateful I am for Your promised return. How thankful I am that eternity awaits. How thankful I am for the perfect plan of the Father, the perfect accomplishment of the Son, and the perfect provision of the Spirit. Help me to be faithful to You as I await Your return. Even so, come quickly, Lord Jesus! Amen.

CONCLUSION

I n the mid-1800s the fledgling republic known as the United States of America had reached a crisis point. Slavery, state's rights, and federal control had combined to form a critical mass of resentment and mistrust that resulted in secession of the southern states and the formation of the Confederacy. The result was the Civil War (or, as it was called in some parts of the South, the War of Northern Aggression)—and the great experiment of American democracy was seriously threatened. The war raged, and it seemed as if the republic were doomed—until Gettysburg. During July 1–3, 1863, the outcome of the war would be decided on the field of battle outside Gettysburg, Pennsylvania. The Confederate forces were on the verge of flanking the federal troops and opening a road to a defenseless Washington, DC. But the contest turned at a place called Little Round Top. Colonel Joshua Lawrence Chamberlain, a college professor before the war, was the commander of the Twentieth Maine Infantry, and he refused to be flanked. Chamberlain called for a bayonet charge down the hill into the face of the rebel forces—shocking and surprising the enemy and winning the day.

The victory at Little Round Top seemed insignificant until viewed in the overall perspective of the battle and the war. In reality, Chamberlain's bold and heroic move may have been the moment at which history pivoted and the United States of America was preserved. The last 140 years of American history hinged on that maneuver—imagine how different the world would look today had the Twentieth Maine failed and the Confederacy had gone on to win the war! So much of history hanging on a single moment and a single decision is an overwhelming thought.

Yet, in fact, all of human history and eternity itself hung in the balance with a decision far more significant than Chamberlain's as Christ chose to take the cross for us. His passion remains the critical event of all the ages, the hinge pin of eternity. Remember the words of Christ to Pilate? "For this I have been born, and for this I have come into the world, to testify to the truth" (John 18:37).

The truth of God's love and purpose for a lost humanity were what brought Jesus into the world—and to His death and resurrection. In His act of self-sacrifice, Christ made it possible for us to have forgiveness of sins and relationship with the Father. Chamberlain's choice may have preserved the union of the states, but Christ's choice to die on our behalf opened the door for us to enter into eternal union with God. John put it this way: "But as many as received Him, to them He gave the right to become children of God, even to those who believe in His name, who were born, not of blood nor of the will of the flesh nor of the will of man, but of God (John 1:12–13).

Children of God! From spiritual rebels to beloved children— all because of Christ's willingness to take our punishment on the cross. My prayer for you is that if you have never embraced the Christ, you would receive His forgiveness today by accepting His payment for your sins. If you have trusted the Savior for that forgiveness, would you recommit to Him your heart, your life, and your service? Recognizing just how much it cost for Christ to love us, may we respond to the challenge of the apostle Paul: "Therefore I urge you, brethren, by the mercies of God, to present your bodies a living and holy sacrifice, acceptable to God, which is your spiritual service of worship (Romans 12:1).

Enjoy this book? Help us get the word out!

Share a link to the book or
mention it on social media

Write a review on your blog, on a retailer site,
or on our website (dhp.org)

Pick up another copy to share with someone

Recommend this book for your
church, book club, or small group

Follow Discovery House on
social media and join the discussion

Contact us to share your thoughts:

 @discoveryhouse   @DiscoveryHouse

Discovery House
P.O. Box 3566
Grand Rapids, MI 49501 USA

Phone: 1-800-653-8333
Email: books@dhp.org
Web: dhp.org